CW00739955

The Pinnacle Principle

Also by Peter Thomson and available from Simon & Schuster

The Secrets of Communication

The Pinnacle Principle

How to Maximise Your Potential

PETER THOMSON

SIMON & SCHUSTER
A VIACOM COMPANY

First published by Simon & Schuster Ltd, 1998
A Viacom company

1 3 5 7 9 10 8 6 4 2

Simon & Schuster Ltd
West Garden Place
Kendal Street
London W2 2AQ

Simon & Schuster Australia
Sydney

A CIP catalogue record for this book is available from the British Library

ISBN 0-684-82126-5

Typeset in Goudy Old Style
by Hewer Text Composition Services, Edinburgh
Printed and bound in Great Britain
by Butler & Tanner Ltd., Frome and London

Contents

Introduction

Hello . . . and welcome to *The Pinnacle Principle – How to Maximise Your Potential.*

First I'd like to thank you for reading this book. Already I know that you are someone who wants to make a positive difference to your life. How do I know that? Simply because you are reading this now.

Let us immediately examine what is going to happen to you as a result of reading this book.

- You are going to be more in control of your life, your actions and your results. You are going to reach the top in your chosen profession, career or life goal.
- You are going to be more creative every single day.
- You are going to be wealthier, whatever your definition of wealth. Your finances will be in order and you will know exactly where your money comes in and goes out.
- You will have the right attitude to life and treat everything that happens to you as part of a great adventure.

In short, you will be the best you can be at everything you decide to do.

How can I make such bold statements? Simply because the ideas, the methods, the thoughts you will read have been tried and tested and proven throughout history. Proven to be the key skills and ways of the achievers in life – those who have utilised the Pinnacle Principle, those who have constantly maximised their potential.

Now, I don't know how soon you will begin to feel happy about yourself. I don't know how soon you will earn the amount of money you desire. I don't even know how soon you will maximise your potential. What I do know is that those who have already begun the process say to me, 'Peter, these ideas are so simple, so easy to implement, such common sense, that they work all the time!'

1 Take enthusiastic action

There is a moment in every person's life when the awareness of their destiny bursts like a bubble onto the surface of their conscious mind. It is then that the weak avoid the realisation and busy themselves with the mundane tasks of their lives. It is also at that moment that the strong will awake and decide to take action to change their world for the better and thereby secure for themselves their rightful and valued place in the history of humankind.

Carpe diem – seize the day!

We all run a company called Me Unlimited

So often we hear people complaining about their lives. Blaming the government of the day, the state of the economy or even the weather. And yet all of us have no real option other than to take total – yes, *total* – responsibility for our lives, our actions and our results.

We can do this by assuming the roles of the most important company. That company? Me Limited, or even better Me Unlimited, a company with unlimited potential to maximise the results of whatever the Board of Directors sets their hearts, minds and focus upon. The whole mental process begins with knowing that you are in control of your own destiny, that you always have a choice – the choice to react to anything that happens in your life however you want to react. This does not mean that you or I have to have a selfish attitude to others in our lives, far from it. By being the boss, by being in control, by taking responsibility we set ourselves up for success and, by so doing, help others around us accomplish their goals and maximise their potential.

If we blame others for the things that happen to us, then we will be at the beck and call of anyone else, dependent on others for our feelings of self-worth or self-esteem. The way we can accomplish our own goals, the way we can support our loved ones, the way in which we can contribute to the society in which we live is to be the boss, the president, the chair of the board of that most important concern.

With that job description come a number of other roles.

The Chair. The chair, chairman or chairperson of the company is responsible for the attitude which prevails in the company. Attitude can only cascade down a company, it must come from the top – from the pinnacle. In so many companies we see the 'boss' treating people with indifference, acting as though the people are just part of the furniture, caring little for their lives and yet . . .

> ***'The way the boss comes in, in the morning . . .***
> ***. . . is the way the people leave at night!'***

Let's look at this word 'responsible' – what does it mean? Often it has been said that responsible means 'response' and 'able': we are *able* to respond. So often responsibility can have negative connotations and yet, with responsibility on our shoulders, there is no room for chips . . . As youngsters we lived with the word responsible used in accusatory questions such as 'Who is responsible for breaking that window?' 'Who is responsible for this mess?' 'Who is responsible for these muddy footprints on the kitchen floor?' Used in a positive way, however, it is marvellous word with many positive connotations. When we take responsibility, we get the credit.

The Sales Director. The Sales Director looks after the income generation of the company, in your company, Me Unlimited. Your Sales Director – you – must have a sales forecast, knowing how much money your organisation is likely to generate in the next 12 months. If you do not have a written estimate of your income for the next 12 months, or for the remainder of this year, decide *now* how much you will earn; for without that forecast, it is unlikely that you will maximise your potential and earn as much as you might like to earn.

The Finance Director. The Finance Director of Me Unlimited – again, you – is responsible for the control of the finances of the organisation and for maintaining a budget and accurate records.

> ***'Many people have too much month at the end of the money . . .***
> ***. . . instead of too much money at the end of the month'***

You can imagine a situation where you and I decided to attend the AGM of a public company because we had decided to invest some of our money in shares. A shareholder at that meeting rose to ask the Sales Director and the Finance Director some questions.

'Do you have a sales forecast for the Company?'

'Do you have a budget for the Business?'

'Do you maintain accurate accounting records?'

Imagine all of these questions receiving a capitalised 'No!' Would we invest our hard-earned money in that company? No way! We would consider those in control to be in the wrong job. It is no different with Me Unlimited: you too are investing in those shares but the currency you are using is your life.

Planning Director. This director is responsible, there's that word again, for goal-setting, for creating direction, for organising the dreams of the company into an action plan which can be accomplished in the time span allotted and with the resources available – in other words, maximising the potential.

Human Resources Director. Responsible in many companies for the people and their well-being. In your company, Me Unlimited, there is only one person for the role: you. The areas of responsibility? Fitness, health, diet, general well-being, motor skills and manual skills of all kinds.

Mental Resources Director. This role, as the title suggests, is to take charge of all mental faculties and includes: learning to read faster, reading this book, soaking up information from every possible source.

Recently, I spoke to a man who reads 25 000 words per minute and I also understand that there are a small number of people who can read at 100 000 words per minute. That's like Data in *Star Trek*, can you imagine it? Well, being able to increase from the normal 300 to 350 words per minute has surely got to have advantages for anyone. All those brain and mental skills are the responsibility of the Mental Resources Director.

Research and Development Director. The Research and Development Director's role includes such things as understanding and using creativity. How we can get all of those creative juices flowing so that our incomes can be maximised and our outgoings minimised, and have fun in every area of our lives.

Communications Director. This Directorship role is concerned with dealing with other people, leadership and teamwork; and using that most important part of our bodies: the tongue. Knowing how to communicate more effectively, creating rapport between the company Me Unlimited and the outside world, including our families, our partners and of course the commercial world.

Administration Director. This Director is concerned with 'time management'. I am not particularly keen on the term time management, as I believe there is no such thing – only *self* management within the time available. However, I will go into that in more detail later in the book. The Administrative Director is also responsible for all paperwork skills and ensuring that the administration of Me Unlimited runs as smoothly as possible.

All in all, nine hats to wear, nine people in one person, nine responsibilities, all up to one person . . . you.

What I would now like you to do is to mark yourself on the following test, out of a maximum of ten points for how well you're operating each directoral role within Me Unlimited.

Role in Me Unlimited:	**Mark out of Ten:**
The Chair________________________	
Sales Director____________________	
Finance Director__________________	
Planning Director_________________	
Human Resources Director__________	
Mental Resources Director__________	
Research and Development Director____	
Communications Director___________	
Administration Director____________	

You may have heard a story called 'Acres of Diamonds'. This was a tale of a South African farmer who was bitten by the diamond bug and sold his farm to search for diamonds. Finally, he took his life in despair at not finding any.

It later turned out that the farm he sold was one of the richest areas of land for diamonds in the whole of the African Continent.

Sometimes, we too can make the same mistake, by not looking within our own acres of diamonds – our own minds, our own bodies, our own brains – to ensure that we are using our talents to the full. I urge you to take the following test. List your talents in the space provided and then give thought to the question: Are you using to the full, the skills and talents you have?

'Are you using to the full, the skills and talents you have?'

This is not to suggest that you are unhappy in your present situation; you may well be making the best use of your talents, and if so then great. However, many people achieve at their highest level when they are using their best skills and when they are doing something commercially or socially that they love to do. With the world itself, we lose the resources and the talents of the world by using them up. With ourselves, we lose the talents and resources by not using them.

Are there skills and talents you have which might be better used?
Only you know.'

It has often been said that successful people make decisions quickly (having collected the relevant information) and then change their minds slowly. Whereas, less successful people tend to make up their minds or make decisions slowly and then change their minds quickly. We have often seen this in operation. The person who jumps from job to job, business to business, relationship to relationship, without giving it sufficient time to find out if they are on the right road, if they are in the right place of employment, have started the right business, have become involved with the right person. My suggestion is that you give it your best shot before moving on. Then and only then, if you realise you are in the wrong place, change! Life, particularly business life, is not a lottery, we don't stand a better chance of winning by simply buying more tickets or starting more and more new businesses. Sometimes we have to hang on to the tickets we have bought until the draw is made.

Think for a moment of the business in which you are involved. Imagine that the business is a hot air balloon, sailing the skies. Suddenly one day the balloon suffers a small puncture, not enough to send it hurtling to the ground but enough to allow a slow escape of the hot air which keeps it airborne. Those in control of the balloon say: 'We must reduce weight, something will have to go.' Would you be one of those to stay on the balloon or would you be pitched over the side because you are too heavy for the value you bring to the operation? If your activities at work don't mean that you would definitely be one of the people to stay then perhaps you should give thought to your current situation and decide if:

1 You are giving it your best shot.
2 You are in the right place.
3 A change is needed.

A look at success

Each of us needs to be in control of Me Unlimited because the '*Principle of Control*' is one of the major principles of life. Being in control means we can diminish stress, increase happiness, maximise potential. You can imagine the situation . . . you are driving down a wide road, three lanes, there is nothing else on the road, you are able to go as slowly or as quickly as you like, you can use any lane you like, the sky is blue, the sun is shining and you are in control – it feels great doesn't it?

However, imagine another situation. You are going down the same road, it is very busy, cars everywhere, you decide to overtake the car in front because you are going about 10 mph faster. Suddenly out of nowhere, another car screams up behind you and hangs on to the rear bumper of your car with only a few feet between you, the lights start flashing, the driver starts honking his horn, you need to get out of the way of this lunatic but there isn't a gap to pull into. How do you feel? Angry, nervous, panicked, enraged? Whatever the feeling, it certainly isn't one of control, it feels horrible doesn't it? Many drivers have experienced a situation when a road they wish to drive down is blocked with perhaps a traffic hold-up or a problem and a policeman directs them on towards a diversion down a road they haven't driven on before. Suddenly, loss of control of the situation. How do they feel? As before, terrible.

Control is essential in our lives, control of ourselves, of our actions, and of our commercial and personal circumstances. This is my advice:

> Take control – be the one who decides the direction of your life. Make that decision . . . NOW.

As you think back over the last few years of your life, ask yourself this question: 'Have I had the successes I wanted?' For a moment, imagine you are 10 years younger than you are today and you are looking forward. What were your dreams at that point in your life? What were the successes you just knew you were going to have? Have you had those successes, or have there been some different results along the way? Remember:

> There are no failures in life . . . only results.

Using the space provided I would like you to make a list of the reasons why you believe you have had the successes you have had, and perhaps why, on occasion, some results were not the ones you wanted.

Did:	Didn't:

If you have not yet added your name to both of those columns, then I suggest you do so. You are the one in control, you are the one responsible, you are the principal player in your life. You and I both need to accept that, individually, we are the ones who make a difference in our lives. There are a number of additional principles that we need to examine and all of them need to be accepted, whether we like them or not.

Everybody sells. The first principle we should all accept is that 'Everyone is in Sales'. Now for anyone not directly involved in the sales business this may be difficult, but you and I know that we are always selling. We sell to ourselves, persuading ourselves to take certain actions, we sell to other people in our lives. We run mental programmes such as: 'Shall I get up at this time or that time?' 'Which suit shall I wear today?' 'Shall I go in the car or take the train?'

Whatever it may be, the decisions you make are all part of selling. We persuade other people all day long to our point of view, we persuade other drivers to let us in at a traffic jam. We hear parents persuading their children to tidy their rooms, a union representative in negotiation for a pay rise for all of his or her members, somebody selling a piece of property or service to another company.

The principle of persistence. You will remember, I'm sure, the story of the tortoise and the hare, the hare racing off and then getting distracted, whereas the tortoise persistently went along one step at a time. Who won the race? The tortoise. Why? Because it was persistent, it kept doing the same thing again and again and again, until it reached the finish line. The hare, who dashed off, got bored and gave up, and I am certain that many people have been guilty of that from time to time – I know I have – starting on a project and not really finishing it. We need to have persistence.

Keep the change. Another of the major principles in life is that of change. We need to accept that everything changes; in fact, the only constant in life is change. Nothing stands still. It moves forwards or backwards. It is very similar to water; water which stands still stagnates, running water is clean and teeming with life. So we must accept change, we must enjoy change, we need to learn how to adjust so that we welcome change, knowing its importance.

I remember hearing some years ago about a man starting a speech and dragging on to the stage an enormous papier mâché dinosaur, over six feet tall. He said nothing to the audience. He then reached into his briefcase and brought out a white mouse which he allowed to run up and down his fingers and then put it back in the briefcase, but still said nothing to the audience. He then turned round to his notepad and wrote in large letters. 'The RC Factor'. Returning his eyes back to the audience, he said: 'Imagine, if you will, that it is 20 million years ago, we have all been asked to place a bet, to place a wager. The wager is this: which, between these two, the mouse or the dinosaur, will last and be around for the next 20 million years?'

I am sure, if we are honest, all of us would have bet on the dinosaur rather than on the insignificant mouse. Well, we would have been wrong. The dinosaur died out. Why? Because of the RC Factor. The dinosaur was Resistant to Change. How many business, how many people, are resistant to change? Yet it is one of the universal principles, everything will change.

There are no failures

The next principle is one I mentioned earlier. One of my basic beliefs is that there are no failures in life, there are only results from which we can always learn. The only way that any rough gemstones are made into a smooth, highly valuable gems is by the application of friction, and that is what life does to us.

It puts pressure upon us, it squeezes us, it polishes us by adversity to become a more *valuable* person, exactly in the way that a lump of coal is made into a diamond.

If things go wrong for you in your life, as invariably they do for many people, just welcome the experience, work out what can be learnt from it so that the experience will have been worthwhile . . .

'There are no failures in life, only results.'

Let us now examine how we are going to start each and every day. I am reminded of the excellent expression made popular by *The Dead Poets Society*: 'Carpe diem (Seize the day).' We need to do that every single day of our lives. Why? Because each day comes only once.

We will explore a number of ideas about this in our time management session later. However, to give you some ideas on how to start the day, the first thing to do is to read your goals, so that you know that each day you are focused to take action towards their accomplishment, the goals you have set for your life, the dreams you have been dreaming which have been translated into goals, so that you have an action plan to be able to accomplish them and maximise your potential.

I think that one of the greatest ways to start every day is to get our attitude right. Well, how can we do that? Simply by focusing on what we want to accomplish.

Some years ago, I heard an American audio presenter, Brian Tracy, say that we should start each day by saying 'I like myself.' When I first heard the idea I thought it was a little over the top, but having used it for many years I realise its power. It is not saying 'I am superior to someone else' but simply I Like Myself. When you are going to work in the morning or doing whatever you do, start repeating this phrase. I like myself, I feel good about myself, I am happy with me.

As my wife often says to me, 'Be the best you can be . . . who else can be?' Be optimistic – and you know the way we judge an optimist. The optimist is the person who looks at the glass and says it is half full, the pessimist the person who looks at the glass and says it is half empty. If we can be optimistic about life, it is amazing what good things begin to happen.

The principle of anticipation

When we anticipate that things will be good, then invariably they turn out well or better than they might have done if we were working on the principle of things turning out badly. I am always amazed, when I hope that good things will come about, how well they actually work out.

Parking the car. The next time you are going to park your car, just believe you will be able to park. My family and I have a great deal of fun with this. On the way to perhaps a busy street we will be saying: 'Oh yes, the people in our space are just walking back with their shopping, they have opened the boot, they have put the shopping in, they have closed the boot and got in their car, they have just started it; now they are waiting for us to arrive.' What usually happens on the way is that someone else is trying to cross the road, so, rather than push past them, we stop and call them across, and when we get to where we want to park – lo and behold! – someone backs out and lets us into a space.

You will find as I have found that the greater the belief of parking, the more likely we are to park. Try it for yourself, crazy though it sounds, and I know you will succeed. I have shared this idea with many, many people who come back to me and report their success with it.

So, at the start of every day we need to be optimistic, we need to be saying 'I like myself, I feel good about myself.' We need to believe that, by looking at our goals, we can achieve something every single day. As Henry Ford said:

> ***'Whether you think you can or think you cannot, you are right.'***

Winston Churchill put it in a slightly different way:

> ***'The pessimist sees difficulty in every opportunity, the optimist sees opportunity in every difficulty.'***

We need to be that optimist, that 'can do' person: 'Success comes in cans . . . not cannots!' If we start every day liking ourselves and understanding that we have to take responsibility, the day has a better chance of yielding accomplishment and success. Success is like beauty, it is in the eye of the beholder, and it is your translation of this emotive word, success, which we will discuss later, which is so important.

On the idea of being responsible, it is a good idea to keep a book of your successes. You could start by listing the successes you've had in your life to date. Many people involved in business keep testimonial letters from clients saying how well they have enjoyed dealing with the company or the person concerned. In any moment of doubt, it is easy to re-read these testimonial letters and get re-focused.

Taking responsibility

Here are some steps you can take straight away:

1 Stop making excuses.
2 Stop blaming others for any failures in your life, not the economy, not other people, not the business in which you are involved, not customers, not suppliers – don't blame anyone else. If there is blame to be apportioned, take the blame yourself; that way you can always take the credit.
3 Distract yourself, so that you have a chance to get your second wind.
4 Set your own standards for excellence. Excellence is a word that is often used in business; let us make sure that we are living it by our own definition and not somebody else's.
5 Let's write our own rules for all areas of our lives. That way it is easier to be responsible.
6 Sell yourself on you again. Make sure you are happy with yourself, convince yourself that you are a worthwhile person.
7 Do a slogan about you. This may sound somewhat unusual; however, if you can have a slogan about yourself, rather like an advertising jingle, then in a moment of slipping off the top rung of the ladder of positivity simply repeat the slogan to

yourself. It might be as simple as 'I like myself, I feel good about myself, I am responsible.'

So, if we start each day with the right attitude, by reading our goals, by liking ourselves, by feeling good, by anticipating the best is to happen, the best of living in the now rather than in the past, then we can be more successful each day. We cannot live in tomorrow, we cannot live in yesterday, physically that is. Maybe we can do it mentally, but we can only live in the now – and if we grab each moment as it comes with the right attitude, it is amazing what we are able to achieve.

IF YOU WOULD LIKE TO RECEIVE A SHORT AUDIO TAPE, WHICH YOU CAN USE AT THE START OF EVERY DAY IN ORDER TO FOCUS YOUR MIND ON WHAT YOU WANT TO ACHIEVE AND HOW POSITIVE YOU CAN BE, THEN SIMPLY WRITE TO ME AT THE ADDRESS SHOWN AT THE BACK OF THE BOOK, AND I WILL SEND YOU ONE FREE OF CHARGE.

Eradicating weaknesses

Now let's look at the other side of the coin and examine what are often called weaknesses. Sometimes I find that people are focusing on weaknesses that are not going to make any difference to themselves. If you have a weakness or weaknesses, or perhaps we should call them smaller strengths or lesser strengths, and if they *are not* holding you back from achieving the major things in your life then ignore them. What difference is it going to make if you change them? This is not to say that we accept all the weaknesses we have. Some of them need to be changed; however, we need to choose which ones to change.

Don't be living by other people's rules. I read some years ago about Steven Kinnell who was a writer for TV series *The A Team*. He has also written 24 other successful TV series – and yet he is dyslexic. What he does is to type up what he can and let someone else correct the typing, or in other words he capitalises on his strengths and that is what we should all do.

If we decide we do have a weakness, then it is best to do something about it.

When things go wrong in your life, and you and I know that things do go wrong from time to time, don't criticise the person, you, criticise the action. For example, let's say you attempt to do something and it doesn't work out quite as you expected. Don't go around saying: 'I'm a failure, it never works for me' or 'Something always happens to me'. Rather, say: 'I like myself, I still feel good about myself, I did not like that particular action I took and I won't be taking it again; I am still the best me I will ever be.' It might take time to reaffirm you love and believe in yourself because it is your opinion about you which really matters. That is not to say we don't care about the opinion of others, of course we do, but our self-belief, our self-opinion, our self-esteem, are so important for getting our attitude absolutely right.

34	96		32	5		21	
56		2	15	55	1	9	6
31	45	8		12	3	41	7
54	53		97	61	4	10	3
56	22		76	43		76	
44	7		23	12		4	
	12	5	76	77	3	12	5
11		19	24	44	2	34	1

I am sure that you have seen tests in newspapers to establish IQ level and the diagram above is rather like these. In this test, we need to work out the missing numbers.

Sometimes we do this to ourselves: we look at what is missing instead of what is there, looking at the weaknesses instead of the strengths, looking at what is not available to use rather than the skills we have. Let's focus on the strengths and if we decide we want to change, then *decide* to change and do something. Here is an idea you can use. Next time you are on your own, take off all your clothes in private, in front of a full-length mirror, look at yourself, and fall in love with you again. Start at your feet and work your way up.

> *'Accept what you cannot change and change what you cannot accept.'*

With the right attitude and being optimistic, you can tackle any opportunity.

Learning more

It is essential that we keep on learning, after all:

> *'The day we stop learning is the day we stop earning.'*

Many people have a number of hours available each day in which to listen to audio tapes, perhaps while doing work around the house or driving the car, and 2 hours a day is 10 hours a week, 40 hours a month. So much time.

Take time in your life to learn more because you can be the headmaster of the school, the principal of the college – you can set the curriculum. Some years ago, on the point of learning, I was speaking at a large sales conference and out of all the sales people employed by this particular large company, there was only one sales woman. She had come first in the sales competition two years running.

At the buffet lunch I met her and asked her a number of questions to find out why it was that she was the winner so often. She started telling me of a course about selling and marketing that she was taking outside the working environment. I asked why she was taking this course as she was already in the selling business, and she went on to explain that the people who were running the course had said the same to her – that she didn't need to take the selling stage because, of course, she was in the sales business and there would be books to pay for. The woman concerned said that wasn't the case, she wanted to take the selling stage anyway. She understood that there was always something new to learn and she didn't mind the expense because she was feeding her own mind. Was it any wonder that she had come first in every competition? No, obviously not.

We need to learn more and more and more, not only about what we currently do, but what we might be able to do, what new skills or new talents we could uncover.

One of the ways in which we are most motivated to learn is by taking tests because, when we take a test, it is immediately afterwards that our brains are crying out for more information. I'm certain that you can remember back to school days when you took your exams; no doubt you handed in the papers after you had finished taking the examination and then some months later you heard the results. Unfortunately, in many situations the results are only in percentage terms, the pass mark perhaps 70 or 80% but the question surely is: 'Which 70%, which 80%?'

When we take tests it's good to get accurate feedback as to what went right and what went wrong for then we know what to change.

I like myself	10 9 8 7 6 5 4 3 2 1	I don't like myself
I'm a winner	10 9 8 7 6 5 4 3 2 1	I'm not a winner
I believe I can always learn something new	10 9 8 7 6 5 4 3 2 1	I believe there is not much more to learn
I embrace change	10 9 8 7 6 5 4 3 2 1	I fear change
I'm enthusiastic	10 9 8 7 6 5 4 3 2 1	I'm unenthusiastic
I take 100% responsibility for my actions	10 9 8 7 6 5 4 3 2 1	I sometimes blame others

I use positive self-talk	10 9 8 7 6 5 4 3 2 1	I use negative self-talk
I do the difficult things first	10 9 8 7 6 5 4 3 2 1	I leave the difficult things until last
I'm just the right age	10 9 8 7 6 5 4 3 2 1	I'm too young/old
I view rejection as a learning opportunity	10 9 8 7 6 5 4 3 2 1	I fear rejection

Total Score = ___________

What is your score BETWEEN 10 and 1 for each pair of statements?

i.e. ‹I like myself› Score 10 Points.
‹I don't like myself› Score 1 Point . . . **OR**
somewhere in between

This test will clearly indicate your current attitude towards yourself.

Suggestion: take the test on a regular basis.

When we're taking tests we need to be careful not to compare ourselves just with others. When you take this test and the other tests throughout this book, compare yourself with you.

You would understand a situation where children might return home after taking a test and say to their mother and father: 'Mum and Dad, I came first in the test!' Well that is fantastic and needs praise, because praise is one of the major things that makes us want to do something again and again.

'Recognition equals repetition.'

What may also be important is the marks scored in any test, because you could come first scoring 37% and 37% may not be the best mark in the world. However, in certain situations the marks don't matter and in certain situations the marks do matter.

For example, in a race, if the idea is to come first it does not matter how many marks we get, it doesn't matter by how much we come first, it's the fact that we came first. If we are comparing ourselves with ourselves and looking at constantly improving, then the percentage marks in a particular test *are* important. In matters commercial, we need to be working harder on ourselves than we are on the job. It's back to taking responsibility for your life and action. When you take responsibility for your learning, when you increase your skills and the use of your talents, then success follows naturally.

The Subconscious Encoding Process

The best garden you will ever have is the garden between your ears, and the more you plant in there, the more is going to flower. The better the seeds the better the flowers and the easier they are to harvest. The garden needs tending on a regular basis, so be careful about the seeds you put into the garden between your ears.

The mirror principle. This idea is based on the law of cause and effect. Whatever you do (the cause), there will always be a result (the effect). If you smile at the world then the world will reflect that smile back to you, if you frown at the world then the world will frown back. If you are aggressive with the world the world will be aggressive. If you are good to the world then the world will be good. We can use this idea in a variety of ways.

Imagine the following situation. If you had a manager in your life – I prefer to use the word leader – who would be the best manager you could have? Well, that person would be someone who could be with you 24 hours a day, who knew what you knew, who knew what motivated you to do things and what didn't motivate you to do things. Someone who knew all your fears, all your dreams, all your wants, all your hopes and all your desires. Who is the best person for that? That best person is you. The easiest way to access that person: a mirror. If you are able to understand this idea of self management and use a mirror to allow you to talk to yourself, you'll be amazed at the results you can have.

To begin with, this may feel a little unusual, standing in front of the mirror and talking to yourself. However, if you stood in front of the mirror and asked yourself, 'Do I like myself?' then what would the mirror say to you? Whatever it said would be the truth and you would be able to look into your own eyes and see the truth of what you are saying.

For example, someone in the sales business could say to the mirror in the morning, 'How many sales calls are you going to do today?' and the mirror would give you the truthful answer. Or if you stood in front of the mirror and said, 'Are you going to keep to your exercise programme today?' the mirror's reflection would tell you the truth, every single time.

In one of my businesses which I ran in Birmingham in England we had mirrors on all the desks of the people in the company so that they could self manage.

Most people don't want to be managed, they want to be led. We are all capable of self management. We know when things have gone wrong and we invariably know what to do about it. We don't need someone else pointing out our faults, we are able to keep to the belief that we are happy with ourselves, that we feel good about ourselves, and criticise only the actions we take rather than ourselves as people. So, use the mirror as your main self-management tool.

A number of the companies I have shared this with now also have mirrors on the desks of their people. Some of the staff use them as rear-view mirrors to see when the boss is coming. However, you and I know there is only one boss in our lives; the boss is the reflection in the mirror.

So, let's go back to the idea of cause and effect. Thinking is the cause, actions are the effect, as a man thinks, so he will be. Whatever it is in your life that you have been thinking about over the years has created the current situation in your life. The current situation is the effect, therefore if you want things to be different you need to be thinking different things. For a moment, think of some of the things that you haven't done that you wanted to do, maybe a couple of ideas. What are the results of that thinking? The results of that thinking are that you may now be deciding on some actions that you want to take to achieve those ideas. What you think about will become the action, what you think about is what you will become.

Where are you now in your life? Are you where you want to be? In order to have a change in your life, it is *you* that has to change, not the environment. So often people go on holiday to escape from their environment. They've never really escaped because they've taken themselves with them.

Life scripting. One idea you can try, and I've tried it, is Life Scripting. All you need to do is, next time you get a quiet moment, get an A4 or legal pad and a pen, go forward in your mind about five years and then write the story of what's happened to you during the past five years (in other words, what you think will happen to you in the next five years). What's happened for you? You are the principal actor in that story. Take as many pages as you like, make it as exciting as you like, you have a choice, write the script and then live the script. You can change the script as you go along in life but at least it will have started to create focus and direction for your life. That is self management, that again is getting into the idea that we are in control, that we are the boss and that we always have a choice.

We need to go into our minds and undertake mental housekeeping, our housework, looking after our brains, our conscious and our subconscious, cleaning out the old rubbish, putting in new ideas so that we can capitalise on our strengths and accomplish more and more and more.

Here are some of the things I want you to do. First, I would like you to sit and have a quiet moment after you've read this part of the book and think of all the people that perhaps you may hold a grudge against or maybe even some people you hate . . . and I would like you to forgive them. Now I know that may seem hard, but if you can get rid of that hate or those grudges from your mind, you'll be amazed at how much clear space you create for yourself. So, forgive all the people in your life whom you believe you need to forgive. You don't need to go and tell them, but you can if you want to.

The other person to forgive is you. We all make mistakes in our lives. I have made mistakes and I know you have made them too. Don't carry the burden of those mistakes with you, get rid of them straightaway, otherwise all that negativity, all those bad thoughts, will hold you back from tomorrow and hold you back from today. Think of the things you have done, analyse them, remember they were only results, and then let go of them.

Accepting our age. We cannot change our chronological age, we can change our physiological age, by exercise, by diet, by the way in which we live our lives. We can change our attitude about age.

> *'If you're good enough, you're old enough.'*
> *'If you're still good enough you're still young enough.'*

Positive things. In the space below list all the positive things about you.

If you can remember the positive things about yourself and reaffirm those positives and keep programming them back into the computer that's in your mind then your subconscious will keep pushing positive things out of that computer, what goes in must come out. If there are things that you may feel are negative then translate them into positive ideas. There is always a positive factor to a negative factor.

Instead of saying, 'As I get older my memory gets worst', start saying, 'As I get older my memory gets better.'

'What you say . . . will be the way.'

Thinking back over the years of your childhood and your teens, you can probably remember the programming that took place for you by the words your parents said to you, the words your peer group said to you, by the words your schoolteachers said to you. Unfortunately, for so many people the majority of that programming was negative. Some of the first few words we hear as children are 'Don't' and 'No'. So many of the ideas that permeated our young minds were negative ideas. 'You'd better not try that, you might fail, you might fall.' It's been said that nearly 70% of our early programming is negative in content and the strange thing is that some scientists say that over 70% of all illnesses in adults are psychosomatic or self-induced.

How many positive programming words and ideas did you receive in those early years? Can you remember any at all? Unfortunately, many people cannot remember any at all. Did your parents say: 'Yes, go for it, you can do it, you're good at that, you'll be a success, I like you.' If not, perhaps now is the time to say these words to yourself.

Other well-known expressions regarding our Subconscious Encoding Process are these:

'As a man thinketh, so he is.'

'You become what you think about.'

And of course the famous quote from Marcus Aurelius, updated by Napoleon Hill: 'What the mind of man can conceive and believe, it can achieve.'

Unfortunately, or fortunately, our brain believes what we tell it. Your brain doesn't care if you're a success, it doesn't care if you're a failure, it just believes what you tell it and does its utmost to bring about the results you say you want.

You and I know people who say: 'I'm always late.' What happens with them? Yes, they are always late. Some people say: 'I'm so forgetful, I'd lose my head if it wasn't screwed on.' What happens with those people? They always forget things. 'That's just like me, I'm so clumsy, I might have known it would work out like that, it always rains on my parade, as I get older my memory gets worse.' What happens? Memory gets worse.

There is so much negative programming taking place, and often the person responsible for that programming is the person who suffers from the results of the programme.

I have a friend called David, who, when he puts an audio tape cassette into his tape player, says: 'I always put these things in the wrong way round!' What happens to him? Yes, you've guessed it, he always puts the tape in the wrong way round. One day when I was with him I said, 'David, why don't you say, "I always put these things in the *right* way round."?' He said it and guess what happened, yes, he always put the tape in the right way round. Whatever we programme into our brains is what we get. We are just like a computer and the computer expression GIGO (Garbage In, Garbage Out) or my version (Good In, Good Out) works every time.

Often we are motivated to change our programming by something outside ourselves, a seminar we've attended, a book we have read or an audio tape we have listened to, and yes, all of those things can motivate us to change the way we live and act. However, unfortunately, there are missing ingredients from that outside motivation.

Outside motivations. Outside motivations are like the sun shining on us, we feel warm and good about ourselves; however, take the sun away and we can quickly revert to our old, cold ways. Or it can be like a Chinese meal, we eat it and feel full, but within a few short hours we're hungry again – what's missing? Well, first the glue to stick the ideas firmly to our brains and minds. Second, in some outside motivation the knowledge of how the brain accepts and deals with information. Third, the Subconscious Encoding Process, the process which uses the appropriate words to fix the ideas firmly. Well, how can we capitalise on all that excellent outside motivation? Let's look now at how the brain controls this marvellous invention, the human being.

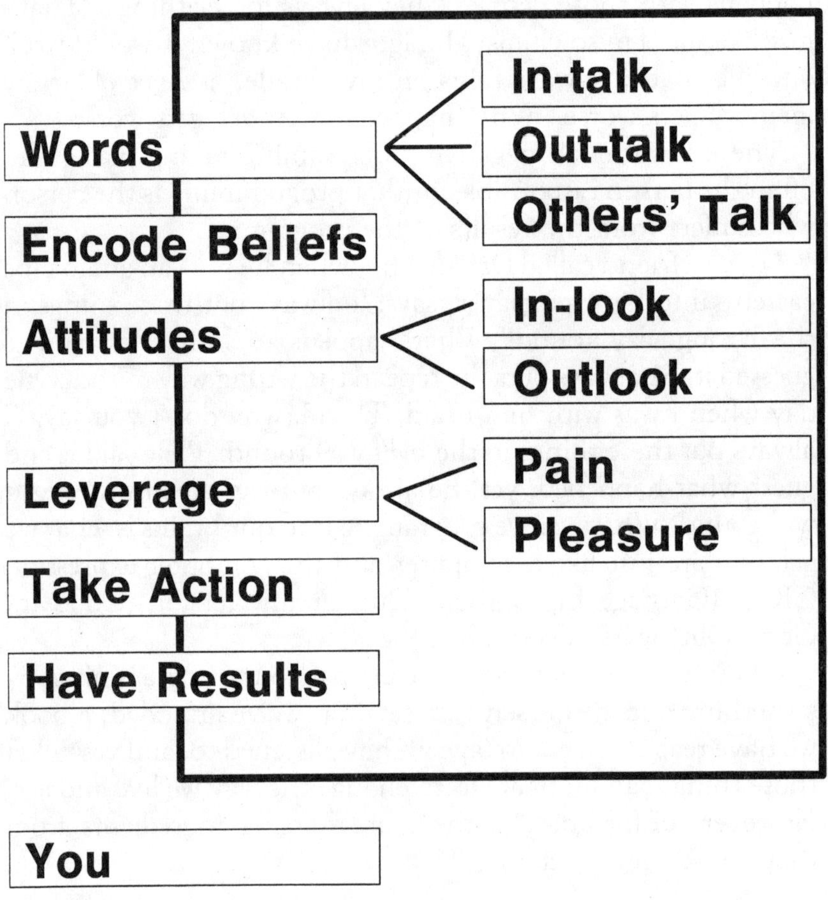

Whatever is happening in your life, whatever results you are experiencing, are as a direct result of the actions you took. Why did you take those actions? You took those actions because of leverage, the leverage of pain and pleasure, you took action to avoid pain or gain pleasure. Why did you have the leverage? You had it because of your attitude, your In-look, your Outlook. The way you looked in at yourself, the way you looked out at the world, and your attitude came from your belief pattern in encoded beliefs which created the attitude. Where did these beliefs come from? They came from the words you said inside your mind, the words you said outside your mind and the words you have *believed* of other people.

So the words you say create the beliefs, the beliefs create the attitude, the attitude gives the leverage and the leverage creates the action. The action creates the results. Sounds complicated? No, it's incredibly simple.

The three stages of programming which normally take place are the following:

- Stage one, negative programming, is the type of programming or In-talk Out-talk characterised by the words 'I can't', 'I'll try to', 'I wish I could'. That is negative programming.
- Stage two, problem recognition, is characterised by the words 'I ought to', 'I should', 'I need to', 'I feel I must'. The challenge with that style of programming is that the problem is recognised but no solution is tendered. The mind subconsciously finishes the programme for us, 'I ought to spend more hours with my children . . . but somehow I just don't make the time.' 'I really should tidy my desk . . . but I know I won't!' 'I need to spend time on my finances . . . but I know I won't do that either'. 'I really must start that exercise programme . . . but . . .', and on and on.

The problem is recognised but no solutions are offered, that's stage two, and it unfortunately creates guilt, worry and, sometimes, stress.

Stage one doesn't do that nearly as much. In stage one we've already given up hope of doing whatever it is we might want to do, 'I can't do it, that's it, give-up time.'

Stage two, 'I ought to, I need to, I must, but I can't find the time, I don't have the willpower . . .' This recognises the problem and creates stress.

- Stage three, taking action. Stage three, on the other hand, focuses on solutions and is characterised by the words, 'I can, I do, I am, I have.' 'I can do those exercises', 'I do spend time with my children', 'I am a happy person', 'I have tidied my desk'.

Now there is a strange thing about programming: it doesn't matter at this stage if you have actually done or become whatever it is. What matters is that you tell your brain *in advance* that you have already done it, or have already become it, whatever it is or might be. Then your brain will act accordingly. It will do everything in its power, and that is a considerable power, to make sure that your programme is consistent with reality.

For example, you might say: 'I am happy.' Note the *am* happy and not *will be* happy. Will be is always in the future and we are not talking about the future, we are talking about now. So the programme is, 'I am happy' and the brain will create happiness; try it for yourself. Say it in an appropriate manner, 'I am happy, I feel good about myself.'

Isn't it amazing how that works in life? Perhaps you might now try saying (in a miserable voice): 'I am happy.' If you do that you do not get the belief pattern, you get a different belief pattern. However, if you say, 'I am happy, I feel good about myself' in a bright positive tone, then you get a happy belief which creates the happy Out-look/In-look, which creates the happy feelings and maybe even happy actions. Perhaps you're sitting up straighter than before, or a smile has appeared on your face.

Try another one (in a sad voice): 'I am sad.' That sad In-talk creates sad belief which creates sad In-look/Out-look attitude, which creates sad feelings, which creates sad actions. Have your shoulders suddenly slumped, has your face lost its sparkle, do you feel down, has your head fallen slightly forward? It's so simple.

'What you say will be the way.'

Perhaps now to get back on track, it would be worthwhile saying in a bright tone, 'I am happy', 'I feel good about myself' – yes, that's better. This will work for all positive programming, 'I am', 'I can', 'I do', 'I have'.

These days more and more people are becoming aware of the effect of positive programming and the power of the principle of positive anticipation. Olympic athletes use what has commonly become known as autogenic training, visualising themselves running the race and coming first. Visualising themselves throwing the javelin and actually seeing it soaring through the air to a new personal best throw. Visualising themselves hurtling downhill on their skis and looking up at the giant electronic scoreboard to see their name in first place, and yes . . . it works. Track athletes do it, skiers do it, boxers do it, football teams do it, business people do it, sales people do it. Mental rehearsing before the action, if they can do it then you can do it.

How and when do we change the programme? Answer: all of the time.

First, whenever you catch yourself saying negative things inside your mind, stop, and rephrase those negatives into positive. 'I'm too old for this' becomes 'I'm just the right age, my age gives me experience'. 'I'm too young for this' becomes 'I'm full of energy, I can always do anything I want to do, I'm just the right age'. 'I always forget people's names' becomes 'I always remember people's names'.

If this is a new way of talking to yourself for you, and you feel uncomfortable for the moment, just trust me and try it for one day, just one day, for you've got nothing to lose and everything to gain. Make a decision now that you are the type of person who says positive statements to themselves and when you hear any of that negative In-talk, rephrase it. When you hear any negative Out-talk, rephrase it. You may get funny looks from people, but no doubt that will make you smile as well.

Second, we need to change our Out-talk – the things we say about ourselves and our circumstances to others – because that is also part of the programme. When you catch yourself about to say something detrimental, or negative about you, to another person, rephrase it. Explanation is unnecessary, just blame me.

As always, we can use the mirror to change our programming. That best manager, that perfect leader, you. Stand in front of the mirror and programme the day, tell yourself how good the day is, how good you are, how successful you are, how happy you are. The fact that you are a 'can do' person, if you are in business that you are a money-making machine or if you are in teaching that you are a fantastic teacher and people always enjoy your lessons, whatever is applicable for you. What better way could there be to start each and every day than reminding ourselves that we feel good about ourselves and the day is wonderful and it's good to be alive? This has got to be a better start to the day than the start experienced by so many people: 'Oh no, it's morning, of to another boring day at the office, no doubt everybody will be in a bad mood, I don't suppose anyone will want to order anything today, the recession probably got deeper overnight, I forget the boss's name right in the middle of my presentation, oh dear it's Monday.'

No way! Cancel those thoughts, reprogramme. 'It's great to be alive, I am a "can do" person, I am happy, I feel good about myself.' You can hear more of this great stuff on the 'Good Morning' bonus tape. Send for your free copy to the address at the back of the book.

Preview review. Another area that must be covered every morning is reading goals. Read your goals aloud to yourself, perhaps even facing the mirror. Later we will cover a simple system for setting goals.

If you are in business in any way whatsoever, or involved in meetings during your normal day, you can also use this next idea for amazing results. It's called preview review. This is how it works. Before going into any meeting, many people would preview that meeting, perhaps just mentally or maybe even on paper. A quick look down the agenda or a brief thought as to what they might say or do.

After most meetings, many people would review what took place, albeit mentally for some or a report format of some kind for others. My suggestion is, before the meeting, actually write a report of *what took place*. That may sound strange, I know, as the meeting hasn't taken place yet. How can you write a report about what actually took place? Just do it . . . Take a few moments as though you have entered the meeting, had the conversation, completed the meeting and are back outside or back at your desk or home and you are writing a report about what took place. Just rely on your brain. What were the results? Focus on results.

What this does it to set up the appropriate pressure within you to make sure that, first, you cover everything you need to cover, for how else can you be reviewing it? And second, in some strange way it increases the chance of the meeting actually proceeding in the way in which you want.

If you are in the sales business you could use this method and I would suggest that you do it before every sales call. It takes only a minute to do and the results, I have found from personal experience, are outstanding. If you are involved in sales and everyone is in *that* business, just try it and see for yourself what will happen. Then you can be the judge as to whether or not you should carry out a preview review on a regular basis. I know that if you do try it, you *will* use it, because it works.

I remember the first time I tried the idea. I was the chairman of a company situated in Birmingham. We found and supplied money for companies to purchase the goods they wanted to buy with leasing arrangements. In effect we bought and sold our clients' money to our other clients. Some clients had money they wanted to sell. Some clients wanted to buy money. We were a leasing broker.

I wanted to negotiate the price at which we bought the money from one of our major clients. As in any business, if you can buy your product a little cheaper and still sell at the same price, your margins and profits increase. Buying and selling money was just the same. It was obvious that the negotiations were likely to be somewhat difficult and tricky, as I had dealt with the Managing Director of the client company before.

Before going into the meeting, I sat in the car and wrote a report to myself as though the meeting had actually taken place, including the full details of the arrangement we had come to at the end of the meeting. It was like déjà vu. Throughout the meeting, it was as if I'd been there before, almost as if I had scripted the meeting, my points, the client's points, the negotiation, the outcome.

Getting back into the car after the meeting had finished, I looked at my preview review notes and was stunned that, down to some of the smallest details, it was right. OK, not every single thing was there, but I was amazed, and more than that I was happy. That experience taught me a valuable lesson, valuable indeed. The results that that meeting produced for the shareholders of my business, when sold for a multiplication of profits, equalled a staggering £900 000. Yes, nearly a million pounds. I don't say that to impress you, simply to impress upon you the power of the method of Preview Review.

Part of our positive In-talk, our programming, can be the Life scripting I mentioned earlier, preparing a Preview Review script of the next five years of your life and then simply living the script, starring in that film.

The positive programme statements to ourselves are often called affirmations and can be prepared in two other major ways to help us constantly be aware of our goals and dreams in life and our expectation of their fulfilment and accomplishment.

First, write out positive programming statements on cards and decide to read them at least once every day. In the morning, for example, the cards could be stuck to your bathroom mirror or on the sun visor of your car (reading them before you set off and not while driving). You could keep them in your wallet or purse or any place where you will see them every day. A system I use is to have positive affirmations written on a small card (approximately 3 inches by 4 inches in size) with two holes punched on the left-hand side. Using a diary system which is in effect a small ring binder with a page for each day, I simply move the card forward and cannot help but read it first thing every morning and cannot help but see it throughout the course of the day as I use my diary or day planner. This card is a constant reminder of my goals and positive thoughts about myself.

Second, write out the statements you wish to make to yourself and record them on tape. If you have an answering machine with an endless loop tape, you could record them onto that tape and then play it a number of times onto a standard cassette player, thus creating a long tape without having to repeat the statements a number of times. If you don't have an answering machine with an endless loop tape then simply repeat the statements as many times as you wish onto ordinary tape. It is best to repeat the messages on both sides of the ordinary tape, and you can easily obtain short tapes, perhaps C30s (15 minutes per side) or even C10s (just 5 minutes per side). There are certain rules for this procedure:

1 On the tape you must use *you* and not *I*. For example, 'You are happy', 'You feel good about yourself'. This is because, in effect, although it is your voice you are hearing from the tape machine, it's as though someone else is talking to you.

2 It must contain no, I repeat no, linguistic negatives. Your brain has a real problem with negatives. As we will see later, our minds think in pictures and therefore our programming must be of the type that our mind can translate into pictures. Can you think of a picture for 'no'? As in 'Don't do something'. It is extremely difficult. Of all the people I have ever asked at the many seminars I run, nobody has ever come up with a really effective picture for 'not'. Perhaps the best one, though, is a picture of the action with a cross placed over it, but that still doesn't really do the job.

A simple practical demonstration. If you are in a place where you can stand up, just do so for a minute and instruct yourself: 'Please do not stand!' I'm sure that if you are like me, you will have a moment's hesitation with that instruction before you sit down. Why? Because your mind receives, in effect, 'Please do stand . . . not', and it is, for a moment confused.

Similarly, 'Don't think of elephants'. It is impossible not to think of elephants, for to avoid thinking of them we *have* to think of them.

So no negatives, or rather: only positives. And of course that includes missing out such things as 'Less', 'Un-', and 'Dis-'. Be careful with this idea, be absolutely certain that everything is phrased in the positive.

3 All of the statements must be in the present tense. Let me explain. If you say to yourself, 'You will be a millionaire', then that statement is regarding the future, 'You *will* be . . .', so each time you say it, hear it or read it it obviously hasn't yet come to pass. It is still 'You will . . .', not 'You are . . .'

Similarly, 'I want to be . . .' is no good either. 'Want to be . . .' is a future statement. All programming must be in the present tense. 'I am', 'You are', 'You have', 'I do', 'You do', 'I can', 'You can'. I know this seems strange. However, we need to create the pressure in our system that says, 'It's happened' although it hasn't happened.

It must be that illogical, in the sense that the desired result is focused upon. Remember, we focus on solutions, not problems. By setting the affirmation in the present tense, we are motivated through away motivation, i.e. pain, either to stop saying the statement or to do something about it.

4 The Programming In-Talk must be specific. There is no point saying 'I am rich' or 'You are rich', 'I am slim' or 'You are slim', 'I am fit' or 'You are fit'. Without specific parameters of the statement, your brain cannot understand the programme. What do you mean by rich? What do you mean by slim? What do you mean by fit? I'm sure if we asked one hundred people the definition of these words, we'd get one hundred different answers for each question.

So make absolutely certain that the words are specific. For rich, a certain amount of money in a savings account, or the state of your finances specifically and with a date. It may not be rich, by your definition, to have one million pounds in a savings account, and be two million overdrawn in your current account. Take into account *all* the factors.

With slim, set a target weight to programme, the fact that you are that weight. In that way your brain will start telling you that there is a problem with four candy bars every day or a bag of salted roasted peanuts every evening with a pint of beer. Be as specific as possible.

If you need to put a date with the target, great, do that as well. Just still say, 'I am or' 'You are' or 'I have' or 'you have', and state the future date.

5 Make absolutely certain that there are no side-effects to the programming by choosing the words carefully. Are you really sure that the statements you are making are giving you what you desire? Use what I call the PETER principle, which we will be using in our goalsetting exercise: Precise Exciting Truthful Effective action and Recordable. The first three are the ones for programming, Precise Exciting and Truthful, and truthful includes honest and realistic.

All of these rules for preparing the tape apply to the written versions of your programming as well, positive, present tense, illogical, specific and no side-effects. Some of the areas you might wish to consider for your programming are: Work, Home, Career, Teams, Leadership, Exercise, Diet, School, Learning, Stress and Travel. I'm certain you can come up with the exact ones you need.

There is one beneficial side to recording your own programming tape, other than the opportunity to play it at the start of the day or while driving or working, and that is its subliminal effect. Subliminal tapes have been around for many years and although among scientists opinion is mixed, there are still a vast number of eminent people who swear to their effects. I understand that it is illegal in some countries to use subliminal messages on film or audio tape actually to sell or market a product or service. However, the technique is used extensively in supermarkets to reduce shoplifting with positive, 'honest'-type messages being recorded beneath a soundtrack of pleasant music. This music is called the masking. However, recent research has shown that unmasked subliminals, messages without the music or crashing wave noises, can work just as well and in some cases even better. This may be because listeners can play the tape first to assure themselves that only messages they want to hear are on the tape.

Well, by creating your own audio programming tape, including the affirmations we've just covered, using the rules I've outlined, you will have created your own subliminal tape. If you are playing the tape in your office or home, use one of those tape players with an auto-reverse, so that you don't have to keep rewinding. Now, simply turn down the volume so that the usual noises of the environment act as the mask, or in the car use the usual traffic noises as the mask by again turning down the volume. It needs to be at a level so that you can hear the sounds but cannot distinguish the exact words.

In view of the conflicting view of subliminals and their impact, you must make up your own mind as to their effect. I certainly use my own subliminals and I'm happy with the results. If you wish to put music on the tape, by all means do so, it's your tape.

Much of the research by the Hungarian scientist, Georgi Lazanov, concluded that music is a great aid to learning. In particular, baroque music at a largo tempo – slow, approximately 60 beats per minute. Students taught foreign languages using the Lazanov method (now often called Super Learning) show incredible speeds of learning with almost total recall of the information. I tried some of these tests with one of my sons and was equally amazed with his retention of a list of French words.

So, to summarise In-Talk programming:

To change our circumstances, situation or results, we must change our actions.

To change our actions, we must create a change in our feelings, or create leverage.

To change our feelings, we must change our Out-look, our In-look, our attitude.

To change our attitude, we must change our opinions and encode new beliefs.

To change our beliefs, we need to change our programming, our In-Talk, our Out-Talk. We can consciously change In-Talk and Out-Talk by catching ourselves and changing negatives into positives. We can prepare written and spoken affirmations to use on a daily basis, in the style that best suits our own situation and comfort. I know that all of these actions will take time, but without them our potential for accomplishment and success is diminished. With them, our potential is enhanced.

Self-management

Now to the steps you need to take to increase your skill and abilities in this most important topic:

1 Accept that you run a company called Me Unlimited.
2 Make a list, preferably on paper, as to why you have had or haven't had the successes you wanted. We will go into the interpretation of the word success later in the book.
3 Welcome change and fully accept that one of your mottos will be: 'There are no failures in life, only results, from which I always learn.'
4 Be optimistic, say such words as, 'I like myself', 'I feel good about myself', 'I enjoy being responsible for my life and actions'. Say them every day.
5 Read your goals first thing every morning.
6 Recognise your 'lesser strengths' and decide now to do something about them. Recognise your strengths and capitalise upon the results you get by utilising them.
7 Use the mirror as your major self-management tool. Get a mirror for your desk or work area – it may seem strange at first but it will be well worthwhile.
8 Become a student again, join the university of life, the academy of accomplishment, decide on the curriculum and accept that everyone around you can teach you something of value. Listen to those teachers, listen to tapes, read books, increase your vocabulary.
9 Decide – that key work again – to spend time just for you, to do that mental housekeeping, forgiving, acceptance of self, a list of negatives banished forever, standing naked in front of the mirror. Remember: 'Accept what you cannot change . . . change what you cannot accept.'

10 Go through the positive In-Talk programming we have discussed, catching the negatives, rephrasing into positives, 'I am', 'You are', 'I can', 'You can', 'I do', 'You do'. Prepare your tape and use it subliminally if that is right for you.

If you do all of these things over a period of time, if you really accept that self management is the only way to accomplish your hopes, your dreams and your goals, then you will justly have the title 'Chairman of the Board', 'President of the Company', 'Master of Your Own Destiny', if, and only if, you take . . . enthusiastic action.

Motivation

A second piece in the jigsaw of accomplishment is motivation. Why are we motivated to do the things we do? And why are we motivated to resist doing the things we don't do? How can we motivate ourselves and how can we motivate others? Let's start with a summary:

1 Outside motivation.
2 Pushes and pulls which other people have upon us.
3 Inside motivation.
4 The difference between drives and needs.
5 Psychological needs.

All of these areas and information will enable you to motivate yourself and others into action, actually how to do it, the methods you can use to get the results you want out of your life and how to accomplish more and more. Discover a simple way to sell yourself on you; find ways in which you can use motivation, with stories of those who have used it; and learn the steps to take so that you will have an action plan ready for use.

Well, what are the benefits of knowing about motivation? If we are aware of what motivates us, then we are more in control of our lives, we are making the decisions, playing by our own rules and deciding who and what pushes and pulls us. By using self-motivation we will get more done and, more importantly, more done of the things we want to do. Less at the beck and call of others. By understanding motivation, we will enhance our skills of leadership and teamwork, or of managing or leading others – and that is a definite advantage in any commercial situation. It enables us to help people involved in our lives truly to get what they want out of life.

In effect, understanding motivation can enable us to satisfy many of the psychological needs that create motivation – a good circle of opportunity – the motivation to be motivated. We have already discussed briefly the outside motivational effect of attending a seminar or listening to a motivational tape. The sun shines upon us and we feel warm and good about ourselves; when the sun moves away, we return to our old, cold selves again. This may be because of the three missing ingredients:

1 No glue.
2 No knowledge of the brain function.
3 No In-Talk programming.

We now have the tools to create the missing ingredients; however, we are fully aware that motivation needs to be an 'inside job'. We need to be internally motivated in order to create a lasting effect. 'Outside' style motivation can be the catalyst to action, but we also experience what I term the 'under' outside motivators in our lives.

Picture yourself as a saucepan of cold water put on a cooker with the gas or electricity turned on. This can have the effect of getting the pot boiling; but take away the source of the heat and the water soon cools down again. The 'under' outside motivation is only short term and must always be used simply as a catalyst to prompt self-motivation. 'Under' motivators include family pressure, perhaps from the spouse to earn a certain amount of money; home pressure to conform to certain rules or regulations aimed at harmonious living; and perhaps pressure to tidy the garage over the weekend, when you'd rather be watching or participating in a sporting or social event. Family pressure might include having to visit a member of your family and that may be the last thing you really want to do in your spare time.

I'm not saying any of these things should *not* be done; we are simply examining the variety of pressures which do come to bear upon us. Pressing problems could include a situation at work – the pressure of performing at the required level creating a fear of getting the sack. (Fear is covered later in the book.) Or it may be that the garden needs doing, lawns and hedges need to be cut to maintain the appearance of our homes, to maintain our appearance as the type of person who looks after their surroundings.

This, of course, is peer group pressure, sometimes known as 'Keeping up with the Jones's'. Peer pressure can work surprisingly well and it is used by many advertisers to prompt us into taking action to buy a certain product. We are prompted to buy because the advertiser has skilfully, or sometimes not so skilfully, shown us others with whom we can identify buying and using their client's product. New car, the new washing machine, the new house, the new TV; often the wish to be part of the crowd, part of the group, can motivate us into purchasing decisions. In commercial matters, peer group pressure can have us taking action that, left to our own devices, we might struggle with.

I've known of some companies running their sales force on the basis of team effort. Each member of the team receives a basic salary and the commission element of the pay structure is based on the team's performance as a whole. It may well be that each member of the team will have an individual target, based on potential of performance, skill level or past performance, but without every member playing their part nobody earns any commission at all. There is little need for the manager or leader of that team to indulge in any of the usual motivations. The team members will more than take care of each other's activity level by fear, praise, criticism and simple group pressure.

I have experimented with this in business and have seen it have some remarkable effects. The downside, or upside depending on your standpoint, can be that team will quickly identify those members who cannot perform to the required standard and lose them. We see this happening in sporting teams – results are based on the combined efforts of team members and a player judged as not performing to potential may soon be shunned by fellow players, and pressure brought upon the manager of the team to replace the offending player. Watch a relay race to see the motivation of peer group pressure. See a group of people at a fairground and see how certain members climb with fake enthusiasm onto the high speed, twisting, turning roller-coaster ride, in order not to be thought of as 'chicken' by their friends. It is often said that we will run faster to stay ahead of the pack than we will run to catch up with the leader – that is 'under' outside motivation.

In some sales teams, I've seen the following. The Sales Manager posting the scores or results of each team member on a large board in the sales office. Then, at the bottom of the board, posting a figure that was the average of all the figures. This clearly made the point to those who were below average that extra effort, extra sales, were needed, if only to be average. You realise the effect this has: as performances improve by those at the bottom, total sales of all the members increase and thereby put up the average. For there to be an average, some must, by simple mathematics, be below average and some must be above average.

This ongoing motivation will again have those who are unable to compete and accept what is happening drop off the ladder, leaving the company altogether. The idea *can* work but it can also have some devastating results. If you are considering using it, be careful and calculate potential downsides as well as upsides.

Debt can be an excellent 'under' outside motivator, as can worry and stress; however, this may cause only short-term action. I am sure we have all known people in debt, and many in the civilised world have come to accept the state as a normal part of everyday living. We have seen those with a debt problem running around taking actions that we know full well will not result in any major reduction of the debt. It is as though they have accepted the fact that the end will come and that frantic activity merely lets others know that they're *trying* to do something.

Worry will create some activity. Many modern day advertising campaigns have promoted the belief that only slim women are attractive. The models are frequently slender; indeed nearly all of the actresses used in advertising day-to-day items are slim. The world is into slim. The worry that some people can experience is that if they are not slim they're not attractive, and in some cases even that they are not of value.

This has seen the boom of dietary foods and exercise programmes across the world – that's motivation. I'm not saying that being slender isn't attractive. However, beauty, like success, is in the eye of the beholder. Slimness has so often been confused with fitness, and yes there is doubtless a certain correlation. But, one of the fittest men I know has had a heart transplant, plays badminton twice a week, canoes, plays golf, plays volleyball and tennis, and has even won a medal in the Transplant Olympics and – he is certainly not slim.

So all of the 'under' outside motivators can be extremely powerful and the catalyst to take action, but that's all they are. The real reason they work on us is the inside motivational effect they start. So, let's look at inside motivation.

Inside motivation. It is often said that you can lead a horse to water but you cannot make it to drink, and how true that is. We've all been in situations where we've described, in glowing terms, the benefit of somebody else 'buying' a particular idea, product or service. It may be that we are simply attempting to persuade another person to our point of view but, despite the blinding simplicity of our view, the obviousness of our accuracy and the power and eloquence of our words, that person simply wouldn't budge, wouldn't change their point of view, wouldn't buy. Even though what we said, and the acceptance of it, would have been so wonderful for them they wouldn't take action. Why? 'Because people only ever do things for their own reason.'

Let me repeat that: 'People only *ever* do things for their *own* reasons.'

People do things because their inside motivation has started to come into play. The chief executive of a large company who obviously understood this principle stated that his job was to build the greenhouse in which his people could work, it was up to him to provide the motivational atmosphere, but it was up to the people concerned to provide their own motivation. How right he was. If you are involved in any leadership role whatsoever, you know that you can provide only the motivational atmosphere; your people must find their own motivation, 'because people only *ever* do things for their *own* reason'.

This brings us to drives and needs, the inside motivators.

Drives. One of the drives we have as human beings is the reflex drive that we see and feel working every day of our lives.

If someone stirring a hot cup of coffee took a hot spoon and touched it to the back of your hand, you wouldn't have to think about taking action, you'd just act, you'd move your hand extremely quickly and you might even take action against the person. Imagine you are watching the film *Jaws*. Towards the end, when the three main characters played by Robert Shaw, Richard Dreyfuss and Roy Schneider are out looking for Jaws, suddenly it appears at the back of the boat from the depths. Roy Schneider jumps – and so does everyone watching, whether on TV or at the cinema. It doesn't matter how many times you've seen the film, this large piece of mechanised rubber, complete with glass eyes, still has us taking reflex action.

These reflex actions are good for us. They make us blink when something attacks our eyes, cough when we have a tickle in our throat, or something gets stuck there. They make us sneeze when a foreign object, such as pollen, for hayfever sufferers, gets into the nose. The reflex action causes us to be sick when we've eaten something that is obviously disagreeable to the system.

All in all, excellent drives to have, the reflex drives.

The other drives come into play in order to satisfy needs. The drive is the striving we do, the action in play, until the need is satisfied. These drives can be flexible and extremely persistent.

Let us look at the difference between, say, a robot and a human being, in relation to the actions that can be taken. Many of the actions we take every day could as well be taken by a robot, particularly these days as the electronic, computerised brain of a robot could be self-learning, learning as we do from our own experiences in life. Learning that a certain action causes a certain effect and stores that information in the memory so that it can take or avoid that action in the future.

The robot could lie in bed, during the night, apparently asleep, none of its motor functions working, just resting. When the alarm clock rings in the morning the robot gets up, puts on its clothes, goes to the bathroom, sits at the breakfast table, goes out of the house, walks down the road, jumps on a train, gets off at the other end, goes to work, carries out the functions of its job and returns home by train in the evening, sits in front of the TV or paints the house or whatever, until a predetermined time to go to bed where it again lies down, shuts down its motors and computers and lies there, waiting for the alarm call the next day.

I'm certain there are millions of people who do just this. In fact it's frightening that so many of the things we do could, and probably will, be done by automatons in the future.

But what makes the difference between humans and robots?

The real difference is *feelings*, such as happiness and sadness, loving or hating, hurting or healing. And all of these feelings can be summarised into just two areas: pain and pleasure. The avoidance of pain and the gaining of pleasure. What I often call 'Pain and Gain'.

Needs. The need is not the cause of the action we take, the drive is the cause and the drive has a dual personality: pain and gain. Now, that pain may persist during the process of satisfying the need and the pleasure may be the anticipation of a satisfactory outcome.

For example, it may be painful to undertake an exercise programme, however many people are prepared to put up with pain for the pleasure of the anticipated outcome; the figure matching the desire, or a fitness level, enabling them to perform at a higher level of sport or activity. Or it may be painful or hard work to redecorate a room or paint the house. People cope with the pain because of the anticipated pleasure of seeing and feeling the results.

We may need food, but the drive is hunger. We may need liquid refreshment, but the drive is thirst. We all know of situations where people need food, but do not eat: hunger strikers in prison, Yogi of the Asian Continent fasting for over a month. They need food, but the drive for hunger has not yet come into force to prompt the action to eat.

Look at the need for air, that essential for life to continue. In fact the real need is not air, it isn't oxygen; the need is to balance the excess carbon dioxide in our bloodstream. So the need is to balance the CO_2, the drive is for air. That's the difference between drives and needs.

So let's examine the prime psychological needs of people so that we can recognise our own needs and recognise the needs of others. By doing so we can be more aware of ourselves and utilise the needs of others to provide a motivational atmosphere and help others get what they want while perhaps, at the same time, getting what we want.

1 *Pride, importance, ego, gratification*

We have all seen, or felt this need in operation. The young child performing a latest trick or skill, accompanied by the 'Dad, Mum, come and look at me!' The strangely dressed individual who, with an air of supposed nonchalance and unawareness of the effect he is having, enters the restaurant while we are having dinner. It's still, 'Look at me!' As we grow from childhood, it is no longer so acceptable to say, 'Look at me!' but we still do the same things and expect the ego gratification. It is not bad to have to have those feelings – quite the opposite – it is one of our prime psychological needs and we all find expression of these needs in a variety of ways.

Pride, it is said, comes before a fall. In that case, we should all be falling a great deal of the time. So cater for your pride, provided it is in the right way. We should be justly proud of our accomplishments in life, but that is not to say we are going to force them down the throats of every passerby. There is the warm feeling inside when we have taken responsibility (there's that word again), accomplished what we set out to do in the best way we could do, and achieved the result we wanted. Pride is good.

2 *The feeling of personal power*

This feeling manifests itself in so many different ways. Spending money is exercising our personal power and those in business who fully understand this can easily exploit our prime need in this area. You will know yourself, I'm sure, of being in a position where a bill or check has been presented in a restaurant, and you've heard yourself say, 'I'll get it, it's my turn to pay.' We've been there, we know that feeling. It's the exercise of personal power.

Showing off our knowledge in any situation is again personal power. Excelling at a sport or using our confidence is satisfying these first prime psychological needs. We should never be ashamed of that satisfaction. Maybe we should be aware that it is happening so that we can be taking action in a way that is acceptable to ourselves and to those whose opinion we value. Twelve further psychological needs, in no particular order, are:

1. Curiosity. The curiosity need – the wish to have new experiences. Why else would we learn new skills? Why else would we take part in almost any sporting activity, from skiing down a new mountain slope to tackling a particularly difficult guitar solo, or anything else: the curiosity need.
2. Love. We all have a need for love, the incoming love of others and the outgoing love for others, love in all its forms and guises.

3 Emotional security. We all need emotional security, the feeling that our emotions are being satisfied.

4 Belonging. The sense of belonging to a group or a team, belonging perhaps to the crowd of people who have already purchased a particular product. That need is utilised by salespeople the world over. When a potential customer is struggling to make a buying decision, some sales professionals would have a briefcase full of testimonial letters attesting to the fact that others had bought the product, used it and were happy with the results. The customer can have the peace of mind, the pleasure, the avoidance of pain, to know that he or she will be part of the crowd, will belong to the knowledgeable group who have already bought. This sense of belonging manifests itself in clubs or associations of all types.

5 Recognition of effort. This is, in some way, a part of the 'Look at me!' characteristic. We all wish to have our efforts or work recognised by those whom we respect. This may the manager or partner. (In the Avoiding Procrastination section of this programme, I again mention this need.) It is the feeling of completion experienced after the finish of a job or effort that is created when someone says 'Well done!' With this completion we can effectively let go of the task.

6 Peer approval. We live in groups of various types, we belong to teams at home or at work. Recognition that we are a member of that group and of the approval from the team is often of vital importance to us: that is peer approval.

7 Creativity. The chance to be creative is another of our needs. This manifests itself in so many different ways. Creative action in the working environment may satisfy this need and prompt a lack of creativity in the home environment. Conversely, the lack of opportunity for creative expression at work may first bring frustration in the workplace and secondly ensure that a person's creative talents are used to the full at home or socially.

8 Accomplishment. Accomplishment is a psychological need; knowing that we can, we will and we have accomplished something of value is a feeling which everyone enjoys.

9 Freedom. We have a need for freedom, freedom of choice, of action and of thought, and are fortunate that in most of the civilised world such freedoms exist. With freedom comes a need for privacy and again we have all experienced the need simply to have a little time for ourselves. Many people obtain their moments of privacy all too rarely, and they escape every so often to the garden, the den, the study, or to a solitary action sport, in order to fulfil this need. The crowded world in which so many people live sees frustration and anger bubbling regularly to the surface when this major need is not met.

10 Success. Success in a financial sense will drive action. Success of course is determined by our interpretation of that word and what may be financial success for one person may be the breadline for another. However, we all have the success need.

11 Self-esteem and self-respect. These are essential for anyone. We need to feel that we like ourselves, that we are happy with ourselves, that we feel good about ourselves. Many scientists have said that it is impossible to have more respect or more esteem or even more love for another person than we have for ourselves.

12 The winning need, the wish to win. The other needs come into play to enter the race, but the wish to win, the will to win, comes strongly into play if we believe we have a chance of coming first. Winning, again, is one of those words that needs translating from the world's definition into your own definition. For some people, winning may be the bronze medal, third place, while for others gold or nothing is the stake for which they play. Our individual translations are all-important to the satisfaction of our needs.

Turning these needs into drives, which create action, is next for we know that actions create results. If you recall, earlier in the book I asked you to think of a number of things that you'd always wanted to do, but somehow you just hadn't got round to. The reason those desires have not yet become reality is lack of the drive, which comes in two categories: pain and gain. Each drive has its own feelings associated with it. Hunger, thirst and air are examples. When the drive is activated it makes us more aware of ourselves and our surroundings. For example, when we hunger for food we are suddenly aware of the feeling and aware of our surroundings, where we are, is there food available, how far is the next motorway service station, how long is it to dinner time? The drive focuses our attention and causes action, the actual actions that our experience will tell us will bring about the satisfaction of the need.

Now when will these drives, all of these drives to satisfy all of our psychological needs, come into play? First, when the need is great – when the feelings created by the need – are great. Secondly when the opportunity to satisfy an upcoming need arises. Again back to the example of food, which I've used to provide understanding of exactly what is happening inside our minds, brains and bodies. As I have said, the drive comes into play when the need is great or the opportunity to satisfy an upcoming need presents itself. We eat when the hunger drive is activated, we also eat when food is available, even though we may not feel particularly hungry, but *know* that we will feel hungry at some stage in the future.

There is another strange factor that comes into play in these situations. When we are really hungry, we will eat almost anything. There have been reports of cannibalism among those finding themselves in remote places without food. But when we are not particularly hungry and eat anyway, we become particularly choosy about what we eat. This is the same for all the drives.

If, in commerce, times are hard, we are extremely careful with our actions and spending money. When times are good, we spend more easily. It has been said that many successful and profitable companies cover their mistakes with turnover, and this brings us back to needs.

We now know the main needs, that in order to create the drive, which in turn creates action, which in turn creates results, we must have feelings, and the only feelings that really do anything at all are pain and gain, because they focus our attention on ourselves and our surroundings, and the feelings cause the drives, which cause the actions.

Motivation. It is all very well knowing about drives and needs but how can we use this information in order to motivate ourselves into action? Imagine you are at the end of a long room standing by a large block of ice, so that end of the room is extremely cold. At the other end of the room is a blazing log fire: that end is warm and comfortable. While you are standing by the block of ice, you are motivated to move away; that is 'away from' motivation, and is often the catalyst to action. As you move down the room, towards the centre, the ice no longer has the same effect upon you, so its 'away from' motivation diminishes. As you continue to move down the room, towards the log fire, you begin to experience 'towards' motivation, the need to get warmer.

Unfortunately, most people live their lives surrounded by 'blocks of ice' always not wanting to be something, stuck in what is often called, 'The Comfort Zone', in the middle of the room, where it is neither too cold not too warm. For many of us, this 'Zone' is the antithesis of comfort: it is extremely uncomfortable just to be in the middle.

This 'Comfort Zone' effect occurs for many people in many different situations. Take the salesperson, for example. He or she starts a new job to earn, at last, the money to pay the bills, money to keep out of debt, away from the cold. Results start to improve and suddenly that person is past the Comfort Zone: 'Wait a minute, I never planned to get this hot'. So they start self-sabotaging, taking only enough action to keep them in the middle, or even start taking actions that will stop sales from happening. They may start getting up later in the morning; not keeping promises to customers so sales are lost; stop asking for the order; or going home early in the day. The reason: they have no goals set, no targets correctly set, nothing in place to get them 'towards' motivated.

> ***'How many people do you know who never achieve the level of success that their level of skill indicates they should?'***

We see this Comfort Zone effect taking place in sports or fitness programmes. The person concerned starts to perform beyond their normal level and the Self-talk, the In-talk programming, takes on the same sounds: 'Hang on a moment, I can't do this well, I can't keep on winning, I can't keep this level of fitness always, everyone will expect me to do this all of the time!' And what happens: sabotaging effects, self-sabotaging activities, until that Comfort Zone has been re-entered.

Now both of these motivations are excellent news. We can use both of them for results, for the effects we want from ourselves and from others. For ourselves we can recognise the 'away' motivators, things such as lack of money, unhappiness with our current level of health or fitness, unhappiness with our current body shape, displeasure at our smoking, drinking or other habits, and recognising them could motivate us to move away from them. However, don't forget – only so far that we are no longer experiencing any pain. NB 'away' motivation is the catalyst for action, but its effect upon us diminishes the further we move away from it.

When dealing with other people, some are more 'away' motivated in their style: these are the problem solvers in our organisations. They are great at moving away from problems and finding sometimes creative solutions to the difficulties that beset all businesses. When they are not working to capacity and we wish to get the best out of them, we may have tried all sorts of promises of reward, without success, because they are mostly 'away' motivated. Go into their office and say: 'If you don't get this done by Friday at two o'clock, I'm going to have to think seriously about dispensing with your services.' It will probably have the desired effect.

For those who are 'towards' motivated in the main, it can be difficult to understand why these 'away' motivated people have to wait until they are right on the edge of the precipice to be prompted into action; to prevent themselves from falling over the edge. But that's the way it is. If you know some 'away' motivated people in your life, you now have some thoughts on how to deal with them, providing the right type of motivational atmosphere.

For ourselves, we can create the 'towards' motivation by setting goals and targets and being aware of the successes and accomplishment we want. (Goalsetting and Success are covered later in the book.) When dealing with others, it is as well to recognise the 'towards' motivated: often the people in sales, the type who responds to the advertisement for 'Self-motivated individual required – must have drive and ambition and be a self-starter'. These are the people who respond well to targets and reward systems, the people who want to be the best, who want to win, who want those extra earnings. If you have people to control, lead or manage, then you can capitalise on both motivations.

Use the 'away' motivated people to solve the problem and use the 'towards' motivated to set the targets. If you have a boss, manager or leader at work, then it would be good to find out their motivational style. Are they 'towards' or 'away'? The presentation of your ideas and the acceptance of those ideas will stand a much better chance if phrased correctly. Should you be focusing the boss's attention on how you are going to solve the problem, or how you are going to capitalise on the opportunity? When you know the preferred style, it is easy to decide.

How do *we* get motivated? The usual situation is that we get so frustrated that we have to take action. 'I'm fed up carrying this extra weight around with me, I really must go on a diet to get slimmer', 'I'm frustrated at having too much month left at the end of the money, rather than too much money left at the end of the month; I really will go and get a job or I really will start to earn more', 'I have simply had enough of being short of breath just from running up a few stairs, I'm going to start that exercise programme and I am going to start it now!' or 'I'm sick of people treating me like a leper and having my clothes and breath smell, just because I smoke a few cigarettes a day – that's it! I'm not having it any more! I quit!!!'

So the feeling of frustration can really get those drives going. The 'I've had it!' and the, 'I'm taking action and I'm taking it now!' can work really well. But we don't have to wait until frustration sets in. We don't have to wait until the ice is freezing our backs to take action. There is a simpler way: DECIDE. Here's a simple three-step process. As with all of these methods, for maximum effect write down the answers that your brain provides and do it on your own.

1 Decide what you want in any situation. This might be as large as what you want out of and for your life, or something smaller like what level of income you want. That we'll call the 'towards' motivation.
2 Decide what you don't want in the situation you are thinking about, what things you don't want to happen in your life, what level of income would simply be insufficient for your needs or desires. That we will call the 'away' motivation.
3 Again, on paper, answer one very simple question, the answers are going to be the drives. Remember that each drive has its own feeling, that the activation of the drive causes us to be aware of ourselves and aware of our surroundings, that each drive causes action. The question to be answered is simple: 'WHY?'

Why do you want this new situation to come to pass? Why do you want those things from your life? Why do you want that amount of income? Why do you want to be slimmer? Why do you want to be fitter? Why do you want to quit smoking? Why do you want to be able to read at 2000 words per minute? Why? Why? Why?

Until you have answered this question, there will not be sufficient motivation to maintain the drive and thereby maintain the actions. The question must be answered in a specific way. It is what I call the principle of the see-saw – that plank of wood over a central pivot played on by children, one at one end, a friend at the other, each going up and down as the weight of the other is increased or decreased by pushing off the ground or simply bearing down. We make use of the drives of pain and gain, the answers must clearly indicate to you and for you what you will *gain* by taking the action and what *pain* will you avoid by taking the action – be as specific as possible. When you write down the gains, don't just write single words, write whole paragraphs if at all possible; and really experience the feelings of gain that you are going to achieve. Make them as pleasurable and as gainful as possible.

Now on to the pain. The pain must be as vivid as you can make it. Really get frustrated with yourself, really hurt, make yourself cry, make it so painful to keep doing whatever it is you are currently doing, or so painful not to do the things you want to do, that there is no option but to take action, and enthusiastic action at that. These are all going to be the reasons why you must do it, and *now* . . . why you will *not* 'might take action'.

Now, in your mind's eye, create a box and put all of these reasons of pain and gain into that box. Go and sit on one end of the hypothetical see-saw, and have a friend (remember, this is all in your mind's eye) carry the box, with difficulty, to the other end. It might take a number of people to lift the box, for the heavier it is, the better. The crowd lifts the box in the air and *slams* it down onto the see-saw. The result: you shoot up in the air, you're off, you've started to take action. The box wants to be so heavy, so full of gain and pain, that when it lands on the other end of the see-saw, you no longer have any choice in the matter, you're taking action, you're on the move. I suggest you use a minimum of five gain paragraphs and five pain paragraphs; the more you can think of the better, the greater will be the motivation. The beauty of having all of this in writing is if ever you should slip or slide from the path *you* have decided to take, a quick review of the of list, a quick hauling of the box back onto the other end of the see-saw, will soon see you back on the right track.

If you are having any difficulty finding the reasons, or enough reasons, write them out to start with, as if you were selling the idea to someone else. Imagine you were another person, selling the idea to you – what good things would you say, what would be the gains, what bad things would you say, what would be the pains? This will prompt more reasons if you are struggling to find the right ones. The idea of writing things about ourselves as though we were another person can be fun and particularly illuminating.

I was once asked to write a short story about what I had accomplished in my life so far and I was really having some difficulty; I was trying to balance between being too modest and being not too modest or big-headed. Then I asked an experienced American writer friend of mine what to do. 'Write it as though you were someone else,' was his simple yet effective reply. You might try this idea, writing your life story to date, focusing on the positives, the successes, the accomplishments. Have fun with it, it can remind you, in the most modest way possible, how good you really are, how many successes you've had.

Another method you can use to find out the actions you need to take to accomplish your dreams, goals, wants, needs and desires is called 'Modelling'. That is to say, to find a role model, someone who is already doing whatever it is you want to do, or someone you believe would be able to do what you want to do. The questions you would ask yourself would be: 'Who would be great at doing what I want to do?' 'What would they do to accomplish what I want to do?' Or if they are already doing it, 'What do they do now?' Then you simply do the same. Take some actions, check what's happening. If you are getting the results you want, keep doing the actions; if you are not getting the results you want, take some different actions.

After we have decided on our actions, we need to do our In-Talk programming, as described earlier. It is essential that the programming takes place. One of the great ways to keep on feeling happy is the one thing we all know: smiling. It is now a proven medical fact that if we smile, we release chemicals into our system that make us happy. It must be the cheapest drug available! And because we are happy, we smile. When we smile at others, if they smile back they are happy, and so it goes on. Watch a procession of pedestrians down a busy street on their way to work: a smile is like a rare ray of sunshine in an otherwise dark and cloudy sky. Smiling in this situation usually gets you a reputation of being mad or on some form of drug; well, we're using our own chemical systems to create the feelings we want. I once read a story where the author suggested you paint a smile on the glass face of your watch, so that every time you check the time you are reminded to smile. I've seen smiling stickers for phones, or car windows; evidently lots of people, including you and me, think that smiling is a good idea.

Let's look at how others have been motivated to success in life, succeeding by their own definitions, that is.

In one of the Sunday papers, I saw a list of people who had worked as waiters and then 'made it': James Caan, Dustin Hoffman, Fay Dunaway, Kirk Douglas, Lily Tomlin, Jacqueline Bissett, Diana Reed, Kathleen Turner, and Raquel Welsh. Then there were those famous movie stars who once washed dishes for a living but their motivation to act, to be famous, to have the earnings they desired, was so strong that they finally made it: Roger Moore, Roseanne Barr, Warren Beatty, Little Richard, Burt Reynolds, Rudolf Valentino and, of course, Ronald Reagan.

Sometimes we are motivated to take actions, actions we haven't taken before, by the success of others: that's modelling. The runners who couldn't run a sub-four minute mile until on the 6th of May 1954 Roger Bannister, a 25-year-old medical student at the Iffley Road Track in Oxford, ran a mile in three minutes fifty-nine point four seconds . . . and, suddenly, six more did it within a month of his success.

Here is a great story about a 'towards' motivated salesman. Once upon a time, there was a company who manufactured shoes, and decided to expand its market by looking at the African continent. The company's most experienced salesman was sent, flow out first-class and booked into a first-class hotel. He arrived at the airport in Africa, got off the plane, and walked out into the bush – then ran back into the airport, picked up the phone and called his boss back in Europe. 'I'm coming home, it's a waste of time here, nobody wears shoes.' Back he came.

The management decided to postpone their plans until some years later, when they thought they would have another try. This time they sent out their most inexperienced salesman. He was flown out tourist class and booked into a lowly hotel. He arrived at the airport, walked out into the bush, ran back in and phoned his boss in Europe again, but he said something slightly different from the first salesman. 'Boss, send three container-loads of shoes, it's going to be great here . . . nobody wears shoes!' It depends whether or not we are focusing on the opportunity or focusing on the problem.

We can use motivation and our understanding of motivation to really accomplish more. We can be looking for solutions, we can motivate ourselves to get up earlier in the day, we can be more confident and have a positive Out-look and In-look on life. We can see accomplishment as a reward in itself; we know that it is a major psychological need. It is always said that a happy worker will do a good job. Some work-study experts now say that a good job, a job that permits the feeling of accomplishment, creates a happy worker. Whichever it is, if we can get that circle moving, and it's what I call a victorious circle, then it is great.

We are now going to move on to the steps necessary to increase our skills in this fascinating area of motivation. As always these steps will enable you to prepare an action plan for your own use, so that the information is not just information, but ideas, methods and techniques you can use on a day-to-day basis. After all . . .

'It's not what you know, but what you do with what you know that produces results.'

1 Use outside motivators for what they are, outside motivators, simply the catalyst to start the process, and then decide for yourself the actions that you *will* take to create a lasting effect. So, listen to tapes, read books, attend seminars. But do something with what you have learnt.
2 Make up the list of the 14 psychological motivators, the 14 psychological needs discussed earlier, and keep that list so that you can review it regularly.
3 Review the list regularly to check for yourself which psychological needs are creating the drives of pain and gain for you. A better understanding will always increase self management and attitude.

4 Think about what you want in life: ice-blocks you want to move away from and warm fires you want to move towards.
5 On paper, write out the pain and gain and build up the weight to go into that box so that you can slam it down on the see-saw and have no choice but to act.
6 Find a role model or a number of role models for your actions.
7 Create a habit of smiling more often.
8 Use positive In-talk – do that new programming.
9 Make your work . . . your play.
10 Decide now that you are confident and that you are capable of taking all these actions.

Being aware of the motivators, consciously controlling them and making your own rules will enable you to accomplish more and more every single day of your life – by once again taking enthusiastic action.

The life and times of Peter Thomson

A story. Having reached the grand young age of 49 years, it has been great to look back and see what's been achieved, what's been missed and what lessons have been learned that will indicate the guidelines and the future shape of my life.

Looking forward I see another 46 years on my time line. It appears I have a sell-by date of the 9th of September 2043. So much to do, so little time. How did I arrive at today – having conversations with you about accomplishment? Let me briefly share the journey with you.

Born on the 10th of September 1947 in Birmingham, in the middle of England, I lived the first few years of my life in a backstreet café. My father, an ex-public school, ex-Sandhurst, ex-British Army Tank Corps Major, had used his invalidity lump sum pension to woo a pianist with more letters after her name than letters in it – my mother. Having had the lack of sense to pick up an electric fire by the bar on New Year's Eve, aged two, my next few years were punctuated with fun, frolic and frequent visits to the hospital to have my hands rebuilt – all OK now. Kings Norton Grammar School in Birmingham had the pleasure of my company for five and a half years, during which time I managed to squeeze four 'O' levels from the British education system. This number was just enough to qualify me for my pre-arranged position with National Westminster Bank PLC.

After one year as the dog's body for the local branches, standing in for missing personnel, I decided that the banking business was definitely not for me. Sales, I thought, is 'where it's at'. Cadbury Brothers Chocolate, in Bournville, England, was the first of a few more companies to enjoy the pleasure of my daily attendance. Through the work ethic learned in the bank of 'work non-stop until you go home', my new commercial day began at 8.30 am and usually finished at 10.30 am. Why the others wanted to drag out six letters and 15 phone calls until 5.06 pm was beyond me, but I was just beginning to realise that different people have different goals and aspirations for life. 'Can I join the sales force?' I asked, having been reprimanded for working too quickly, too often, too well (my perception of the situation). 'No, you are far too young.' 'Goodbye'.

So I went off to learn the stationery trade, selling carbon paper, typewriter ribbons and odds and ends on the telephone in the heart of Birmingham. Little did I realise the trickery and chicanery that went on in some small businesses. However, I stayed the course for ten months (nine months, 30 days and four hours longer than most) and feel that this period of my life taught me more about business than I would have learned in many years in a larger company. I set up my own stationery company called Danek and Co., determined to prove to the commercial world that the honest selling of carbon paper could succeed. How wrong can you be, but I learned a lot. Danek & Co., I hear you say, where on earth did that come from? Well, if a company can grow to be a multi-million-dollar multi-national organisation with a name like Kodak, then why not Danek? Now I know why. Back to the world of employment.

Diversey Limited, an American company with over 300 sales people in the UK, had the pleasure of my unbelievable workrate for about ten months, working Worcestershire and Herefordshire, selling cleaning chemicals to the food industry, cafés, clubs, pubs, hotels, colleges and factories. Beautiful countryside in the summer months. Basic salary of £20 per week, £6 expenses regardless of how much you spent or how many miles you did. I did about 1 000 miles a week – it was bliss, but not for long. I still had that self-employment bug.

After a few months with a small firm of private investigators, I decided this was it. The next Simon Templar, the next James Bond. Peter Thomson, Private Dick! I can remember the day so clearly. Second of the second 1972 (2 February 1972), Corporation Street, Birmingham City Centre, 200 square feet of office, wall-to-wall lino, one kettle, two desks, two chairs and two phones. The desk I had purchased from the local bailiff on the ground floor – price £1 if he helped me to carry it to my new empire on the fourth floor, no lift – or 50p if I carried it myself. I paid the 50p and carried it. I learned one of the best lessons of my commercial life – it is no good being able to sell things unless you can buy them at the right price. The real journey had started, the base had been formed that was to become the platform for the next 25 years of commercial success. Of course there were a few failures along the way, although these days I never use the word failure, only results. It is my firm belief that there are no failures in life, only results, only lessons to be learned along the way.

Within two short years we were the largest absconder-tracing organisation in the United Kingdom, possibly in all of Europe. We attempted to trace 4 000 people per month for our clients. The clients' list read like Who's Who?: Dunn & Bradstreet, Barclaycard, Barclays Bank, Cadbury's, Mars, Rothman, Imperial Tobacco, United Biscuits, Nestlë, Coca Cola, Schweppes, Littlewoods, Wigfalls, and more and more. Heady days, good staff, great people, great fun. I remember the time when we tried to get all the tracing work from one particular credit card company. 'Sorry,' they said, 'but we have to use three different agencies.' Try as I might, I just couldn't get them to budge. A little bit of sniffing and I came up with the names of the other two agencies they used. Fortunately the activities of the other two were centred on the money collection side of the business and not particularly on the tracing side. I persuaded both of them to use my tracing services. I did all of the work for the credit card company and they never, ever knew.

The business continued to grow and I expanded into bugging, debugging and in-depth investigations – it was great. We manufactured recording briefcases and sold them in high numbers for high profits. Local press and TV became interested, as expected, and I had an excellent, albeit shortish, ego trip with radio, TV and press interviews.

In 1979 I became interested in car phones, the early push-to-speak type. British Telecom approval with such a limited area of operation was to make it *almost* not worth the investment. I obtained an agency and began selling phones as fast as I could. It was at this time I met a man who was to change my life. He was a leasing broker and he explained to me the vagaries of the leasing industry and how goods were sold on lease.

'Surely what you are suggesting cannot be right, John?' I said. 'How will a leasing company pay more for the goods than the customer will pay?'

'They are not buying the goods, they are buying a rental stream of payments,' he explained.

So away I went, easily selling a car phone a day with £1 000 profit in every one, £20 000 per month, so easy, and the customers loved the product. Of course these were still the days when the only cars that had car phones were Rolls Royce, Mercedes and the like. I developed a fabulous sales method, either on foot or in the car. I would approach people who were just getting into the Mercedes or Jaguar and say: 'Er, excuse me. Could I borrow your car phone?' 'I haven't got a car phone' was the reply. 'Funny you should say that . . .'

I've lost count of the number of phones I've sold from that opening line and the customers loved it because we would talk about it after the phone was installed.

My first dabble in mail order came next, through other car phone dealers, of whom only about 60 in the country knew about the concept of leasing. 'I bet they don't,' I thought. So I designed a mail shot in which I said I would pay the dealer a profit of £500 per phone instead of his usual mark-up of £300 if he used my leasing system. The response, 48%. Yes 48% replied and wanted to use the system. It was incredible, £500 for just dealing with the paperwork. The germ of an idea had been planted in my mind.

I knew that cellular phones were then on the way in, so I decided to take a good look at the market. If these cellular phones are as good as everyone says, then more people will want one. If more people want one it will create a market and more people will start to sell them. If more people start to sell them the market will get competitive and the price will fall. If the price falls, more people will buy them and so on and on and on. Do not pass go, do not collect your £500. I decided it was time for me to leave the car phone market to those who wanted to play, and bingo, the thought of lease broking that had been planted as a germ of an idea in my mind sprang into full bloom.

In January 1984 I approached all of the leasing companies with whom we had been dealing via the car phones and asked them if they were happy to take other goods on the same basis. 'Yes' was their reply. Full capital allowances were still available in the United Kingdom and tax shelter leasing was still very busy. I didn't know what tax shelter leasing meant at this stage. I didn't know what rates of interest to charge either, but this was a help not a hindrance. Compass Leasing was born, on the 2nd of February 1984, just 12 years after the start of the investigations business which, by then, I had sold to the staff.

The new baby burst into the world of commercial finance. The beauty of ignorance of leasing rates and terminology meant that none of my staff were 'rate conscious', that is to say price conscious. We would sell our services purely on service, purely on fun, purely on personality because we were always expensive but great to deal with. Month One fees £500, mmm! Month Ten fees £35 000, wow! Month Fifty-Nine fees £255 000, and yearly fees of over £3 million; pre-tax profits approaching half a million, a freehold building worth half a million pounds, 14 000 square feet owned outright, 65 happy, hardworking people and half a million in cash in the company's bank account – we'd made it! In five short years we had made it! Was it hard work? Yes! Was it good fun? Yes! Sales training and personal development training every week, how else would we have succeeded? Professional footballers practise five days a week just to be in front of the customer for 90 minutes, professional golfers hit thousands and thousands of balls to hit less balls in every round. All professionals practise. We practised and kept on scoring. It was probably over this five years of the formation and building of Compass that I learned more about selling than at any other time in my life. We sold items ranging from a lease for a photocopier at £1 000 to a lease for a generator at half-a-million pounds. Substantial profits were made, substantial lessons learned and substantial new businesses formed from the spin-off of leaving staff who set up on their own after the company was sold.

I felt it was time to sell; as I once heard, the knack isn't knowing when to start a business, it's knowing when to sell it. After months of negotiation with a variety of companies, a main board London-based corporation put in a bid – short form report, long form report, accountants crawling all over the place. Finally, in London, in the offices of a major stock-holder, we had sold it, £4 200 000. £2.6m at the front end; a million in cash, £1.6m in shares, and £1.6m after one year, subject to performance. The pools win had finally happened. Then, disaster! Halfway through the year we lost a major client. A large finance company that took a hefty chunk of our business decided to move out of the leasing marketplace. Another invaluable lesson learned which I now practise regularly as '*The Yesterday's Road*' philosophy.

In September 1989 (we had sold in February 1989), I called a meeting of the directors. Image, if you will, that it is now the 31st of March 1990, the earnout year has finished and we have missed it, we haven't hit the figures, we are not going to get the extra £1.6 million. 'If only I had . . . we would have done it.' What are those dots, do a report now? Within half an hour I had those reports, and, adding in my own ideas, I prepared an action plan for every single day of the remainder of that earnout year – a page for every single day. Sure enough, it worked and we hit the target. I have used that same idea time and time again, to tremendous effect. We got paid the earnout and the following year was something of an anticlimax for me.

I hadn't worked for someone else for 18 years and it wasn't easy. I remember going to Devon, on the south coast of England, on holiday – we had bought a small house there as a holiday home, after the sale of the business. The phone rang, it was the MD of the group, my immediate boss.

'Where are you, Peter?'

'You know where I am, Bernard, you just rang me,' I said with a smile on my face.

'I know that,' he said, 'but what are you doing?'

'I am on holiday,' I said.

'How long for?'

'Just for August,' I gently replied, 'I always take August off.'

Now Bernard committed what I believe is the cardinal sin when dealing with entrepreneurial people.

'It doesn't say in your contract that you can take August off.'

'I know, and it doesn't say that I am going to work at 7.00 am, or that I can stay there until 7.00 pm or take work home at the weekends, but I do that as well. Goodbye Bernard, I'll see you in September.'

I feel, with hindsight, that this moment was probably the catalyst in my wanting to leave the company. Anyway, in February 1991, with just two years left to run on my contract, I persuaded the main board to buy me out of that contract for a further golden goodbye. I remember my leaving speech to the fantastic staff of Compass.

'Although I am leaving, I am still a major shareholder. So although I have worked for the past two years for the members of the board, they now work for me.'

Throughout the months of 1991 that followed, I saw the main company's share price fall, and fall, and fall, until my previous holding, worth in the area of £3 million, lost over nine-tenths of its value while I was still bound by a restrictive covenant on the sale of the shares. However, there are no failures in life, there are only results.

What to do now, I thought. Perhaps the area in which I had always had the greatest fun was training, perhaps the area in which I'd always managed to have the greatest impact on other people was training, perhaps the area in which I had always had the greatest success was training . . . Training was to be the way forward. Well, what type of training shall I do? The training which works; self-development training, sales training, marketing, works skills, life skills, and management training with entrepreneurial enjoyment.

And here we are, 38 audio programmes written and recorded and selling well, three books written and published, Results International plc – a joint venture with Nightingale Conant – and running and making a real difference to other people's lives. In-house and open seminars going superbly.

Happily married to my lovely wife, Sharon, with four happy, healthy sons and . . . conversations with you about accomplishment . . . how we can accomplish more and more every single day of our lives.

What more could I ask out of the life and time used so far?

Chains and fears

Fear, I've seen written as False Evidence Appearing Real or F.E.A.R., or Forever Expecting Awful Results or Face it Evaluate it Analyse it and Reject it – all pretty good acronyms.

By chains, I mean the brain-chains; the thoughts that shackle us to ideas we may have of ourselves, or ideas that others may have of us, which are no longer appropriate for what we really want out of life and, unfortunately, may be holding us back.

We are going to look at beliefs, particularly those called self-limiting beliefs, and five major ways in which we can change them.

We will examine rules and regulations, societal-set rules and self-set rules and find ways to rewrite those statute books in our favour, so we can accomplish more of what we want. And then fear; the ten common fears that people have and a ten-step plan to overcome them.

Well, how will you benefit from all of this? First, by recognising the chains that hold you back (and, by the way, everyone has them). Then you will be able to decide which ones to keep and which ones to throw away. Second, you will have a proven way to throw away the old ones you don't want to keep. And third, you will have your own rules for life, and that is going to take a weight off your shoulders. Fourth, you will be able to use your fear for self-motivation and conquer fears that have been holding you back. If we can accomplish all of this, then we will be doing what we are here to do; accomplish. To maximise our potential.

The chains that we have in our life can be a help or a hindrance, depending on the type of chains they are. Some of these chains create a strength in our character, or a strong belief. Some of the chains hold us back from accomplishing the things we wish. The chains are, in effect, the beliefs that create limitations, which is why they are often called 'Self-Limiting Beliefs'.

The Pike Syndrome. Some years ago, I was fortunate to see a video entitled *The Pike Syndrome*. Let me describe to you what happened. The researchers had a large tank of water in which they had a large jack-pike. They put some minnows into the tank and the pike ate the minnows – no surprise.

Then they removed the pike and put it into a holding tank. Into the first tank they put some more minnows, but this time they covered them with a large glass dome. The pike was re-introduced to the main tank, and although it could see the minnows it couldn't get at them. It swam around for some time trying again and again, and when finally the researchers believed it to be the right time they slowly and carefully removed the glass dome. Although the pike could now get at the minnows, it didn't. The researchers left it to the point where the pike died.

The moral of the story: very often what we want is just in front of our faces; however, past beliefs hold us back from recognising the opportunities. These beliefs we can call chains, for they are the self-limiting beliefs that prevent us from accomplishing what we wish to do with our lives. They are the glasses through which we see the world and the colour of those glasses, whether rose-tinted or dark or gloomy, depends upon our beliefs. So often our parents can give us those chains, our peer groups can give us those chains, all of the In-talk programming we have carried out over our lives will have given us those chains. Often people give us chains for all the best reasons, but they are chains nevertheless.

Teachers at school give us chains, they have such a powerful influence on young minds and, unfortunately, some of them do not realise the power they wield. Some years ago, I was invited to The Annual Midlands Region Institute of Bankers Dinner, held in an extremely large hotel. The room contained over thirteen hundred people in dinner suits and long dresses. One of the after-dinner speakers was a local businessman, an estate agent, who had done well in commercial life.

His speech was full of humour and focused on attitude and the effect of other people upon our lives. He recalled that his father, who was now deceased, had always been extremely supportive of all of his efforts. His schoolteacher, on the other hand, had always been critical, telling him on a regular basis that he would amount to nothing. He concluded his story by saying: 'Well, here I am, guest speaker at The Institute of Bankers Dinner, I know my father would have been so proud. I wish he and my schoolteacher, Miss Gibbons, were both alive to see this moment, however, I would like to say a few words to them both.' Looking upwards, he continued: 'Dad, thank-you, Miss Gibbons, **** !!' Then he uttered one single, but extremely expressive, swear-word.

The place fell about laughing, as you can imagine, and his point was not lost on me, as I am sure it is not lost on you: we need, at times, to ignore the comments of those who would put us down, or those who would try to programme us with negative 'Cannot Do' statements. The experiences we have had are sometimes the chains that bind us, the experience that we tried to do something, but didn't quite succeed, and sometimes the memory of that experience will hold us back from trying again – and yet, yesterday is not today.

What happened yesterday will not necessarily happen today or tomorrow. Avoid thinking that because you've tried once and it didn't turn out the way you wanted that it will always be the case. Most successful people have as many so-called failures as they have successes. Look at any successful sportsman, or sportswoman, and you will see that they miss the target more often than they hit it; however, they keep on trying, they know that yesterday is not today, that so-called failures are only results, from which we can always learn.

Remember when you were young? If you were like me and many people I know, you probably didn't like green vegetables – why did our parents want us to eat that stuff? How could they sit there and say that spinach, sprouts, cabbage and broccoli were great, tasted superb . . . they were awful! Can you remember those occasions?'

And yet here many people are today, as adults, relishing those vegetables and telling their own youngsters how great those vegetables can be, as the children pull long faces and think, as we probably did, that Mum and Dad must be mad. Time changes our views. Perhaps there was a day when you didn't like wine, or perhaps only sweet wine, while now your taste has progressed to the driest Chablis you can find. Time changes our views and tastes. As it works for food and drink, it can work for many other things as well. Just try that 'spinach' of life again; this time you might find that you like it.

We all grow as time passes, not just in experience, not just in height, but in ability as well. Things that seemed impossible to do yesterday seem so simple to do today, and if we don't move up and don't move down we stagnate. Nothing ever stands still – change is the universal principle. We cannot live in yesterday, so why try? Don't live with yesterday's chains, test them again and see if they break.

Where else do these chains come from? They come from criticism; self-criticism and the criticism of others. We often learn our chains from the attitudes of others; they tell us something isn't possible and we accept it as the truth, even though it may not be so. The only way to find out is to try it for yourself. People often say that you must have a 'fall-back' position – a position you can fall back on if you (and I hate to use the word) fail. I've always found that people with a fall-back position do just that: they fall back. I am sure that many people involved in the sales profession have had people say to them: 'If you are going to get a job in sales, it's going to be hard and you better get another job or profession or trade to fall back on.' Surely if we start on any adventure believing that we will fail, that is what's likely to happen? Now this is not to say that we aren't prudent or careful, but we must wholeheartedly believe that we can succeed.

My eldest son, James, attended a good school. There was an exam to pass to get into the school and then fees to be paid as well. After the standard five years he took his GCSE exams and received 13 passes – a bright young man. He then started his A-level course, and just over three months into it he came to me and said he wanted to leave school.

'What do you want to do?' I said.

'I want to be a rock guitarist.'

'A rock guitarist eh? Well, have you prepared a plan for this? How are you going to do it?'

'I don't know.'

'Well, come back to me with a plan.'

He did, and then I asked again: 'What do you *really* want to do?'

'I want to leave school and become a rock guitarist,' he said.

'OK,' I replied, 'do it.'

And he did.

People said to me, 'But surely he needs a proper job to fall back on.'

'A proper job, like Paul McCartney, Eric Clapton or Bruce Springsteen, you mean?' was my reply.

When I tell that story at seminars, people look aghast at me, as if I'd gone mad; perhaps you're thinking that too. However, we cannot live our lives through our children, we cannot expect that they will do the things that we wish we had done. They are growing up in a completely different world from the one in which we grew up. Each person has a role to play and the best person to decide upon that role is the individual concerned. I know that this may seem a strange attitude to life, but there is always a chance to take A-levels later on – there are plenty of mature students about. It is far better to have tried to be a rock guitarist, or whatever the dream, than to be numbered among the thousands who say: 'I could have done that . . . but didn't.' Or: 'I could do that . . . but don't.'

If we are going to do something, we owe it to ourselves to give it our best shot, really to try to succeed; that way, when we look back on our lives, we won't be saying that most painful of expressions, 'If only I'd . . .' I really do believe that this is one of the most painful things that can happen to us: to reach any age in our lives and say, 'If only I'd . . .', 'If only I'd left school at that age', 'If only I hadn't left school at that age', 'If only I'd started that business', 'If only I'd married that girl', 'If only I hadn't married that boy'. It's the 'If only I'd . . .' that really hurts.

Some years ago, while speaking to an aircraft pilot, he confirmed for me that the only way to get a plane off the runway is with the throttle wide open, one hundred percent, all out thrust and effort. At ninety percent the runway just becomes a motorway, because the plane never takes off. However, once it's airborne the throttle can be eased back and momentum carries it along. It's exactly the same with life, whatever we decide to tackle; having properly planned for the major things, we must give it our best efforts, we must put our pedal to the metal, full throttle, that's the only way we can, or could, do whatever we've decided upon. Only ninety percent effort will leave us frustrated and still on the motorway of life.

Criticism can also create so many problems. Criticism from others can generate low self-esteem and a lack of ability to say that most important word, 'No'. How many social engagements have you been getting ready for in life, only to be saying, as you were getting dressed, 'I wish we weren't going to this', 'I'm tired, I'm busy', 'I should never have agreed to go'?

Why? Well, one possible reason is low self-esteem, low self-respect. Because we are seeking the approval of others, we sometimes say 'Yes' when we mean to say 'No'. And it's hard to say 'No' to people we like, it's hard to say 'No' to those whose company we do enjoy, because it can lead to feelings of guilt: 'I really should have said "Yes".' Unfortunately, this can lead to us being manipulated by others.

You hear this low self-esteem in the In-talk Out-talk programme. Some people are unable to accept a compliment paid to them. They say: 'Oh, it's nothing, you really shouldn't.' If someone pays you a compliment, simply say 'Thank-you'; you probably won't get any compliments in life that you don't deserve, so accept them with grace.

You hear people say: 'It always happens to me, I'm always clumsy, I never remember names, my memory isn't what it used to be, why does the boss always pick on me, I'm always late, the car never starts for me, I'm too old, I'm too young.' All of that In-talk Out-talk we discussed before – low self-esteem. While we are on this point about being too old or too young, I was listening to a radio programme one morning in the car (I'd just turned over an audio tape) and at 7.50 there was the five-minute slot entitled 'Thought for the day'. The speaker was talking about age, and I thought he had some good points to make. He said that he had been taken to the studio by chauffeur-driven car and that the chauffeur, a man in his late forties, was saying that, after he had been made redundant, he couldn't get a job back in engineering – his main love – and so he had ended up chauffeuring. The chauffeur believed that he was on the scrap-heap of life at only 49 years of age. The speaker commiserated with the man and had been telling the story to the boss of a large company, who then put forward the company's point of view. The chief executive said that for every job they had advertised, they had received over 200 applicants and they spent so much money on job selection procedures, such as psychometric testing, numerous interviews and the like, that they simply couldn't afford to interview every single candidate, so they picked the top twenty. 'How do you pick the ones to interview?' the speaker had asked. 'Well, I know perhaps we are wrong, but we pick the youngest, best qualified. We could have, as well, used colour of hair or height, but we pick the youngest with the most appropriate qualifications.'

And yet the CEO went on: 'When I'm dealing with other people, I don't usually care how old they are or what qualifications they have, I care more about what they can do. For example, on the social front,' he said, 'I don't know how old or how many qualifications our local plumber has, I just know he's the best plumber we've ever used. I use one lady that we deal with at home,' he continued, 'who's in her mid-70s and blind, yet she's the best piano-tuner I've ever met.'

The second part of the speaker's 'Thought for the day' was on the same theme. He told of a young man in the acting profession who was filling in an application form to send to the director of a local theatre company. The young man's father was looking over his son's shoulder and exclaimed: 'What about all those qualifications you got at that incredibly expensive school I paid for, you haven't mentioned any of those?' 'Dad,' the young man replied, 'the director isn't interested in the slightest in my qualifications, in what I've learned, he wants to know *what I can do.*'

What lesson can we learn from this? I think it is the following: if we are in business and contemplating taking on more people, before we decide on the selection procedures, maybe, just maybe, we could ask some other people what they think. And the people we could ask could be those who work with us, the people who are going to work with the new person. And, if the job involves contact with the company's customers, how about asking the customers? Could it be that the majority of people want to deal with younger or older people? I don't know, but customers know. Is age really that important? Only to the person who has age as a problem.

OK, so here are five methods you can use to break free of these chains:

1 *Love and understanding*

The way to use the method of 'The Eyes of Love and Understanding' is to sit quietly and think about yourself and what self-limiting beliefs you may have. Then, in your mind's eye, imagine that you are another person, a person who loves you, a person who has an understanding of you, a parent, a spouse, a trusted and close friend, someone who always sees the best in what you do. What would they think about this self-limiting belief, this chain, what would they say to you about this situation? I am certain that their love and understanding would create a different view.

Visualisation is discussed later in the book, so for the moment just think about creating mental pictures – your mind is quite capable of doing it. You could carry out this exercise on paper, simply writing out what the other loving and understanding person would think, would feel, would say to you, and after doing so, or doing the visualisation, just maybe you will believe that the situation is not perhaps as you thought.

2 *Programming*

We have already discussed the power of the In-talk programming within the Subconscious Encoding Process. Take those negative beliefs, those negative chains and reprogramme them into positives. For example, change 'I never remember faces' into 'My memory is getting better and better'. Change 'I'm always late' into 'I'm always on time'.

3 *The Viking Principle*

I've often heard this story about the Vikings. When they set off on their journeys to plunder other lands, there was one thing that the commander of each ship ordered: immediately on landing on enemy shore, they were to burn the boats – yes, the boats they'd just arrived in – because then there would be no way back without victory.

It is amazing how focused we become when we have no choice as to which direction to go. If there is only one road, we might as well travel it with a glad heart and with all our efforts.

So, if there are chains in your life, situations that are holding you back, burn those boats and give it your best shot, knowing there is no choice.

4 *The Shatter Method*

You will need a quiet moment on your own to utilise this method. Sit and imagine a picture of you as you want to be, strong, without the chains that are holding you back from accomplishing whatever it is that you want to accomplish (you can use the method for any situation where the chains have come to bear), but possessing the skills you need, the Out-look In-look attitude, in control. See yourself and feel yourself breathing deeply, quietly and totally confident.

Now shrink that picture, in your mind's eye, into a small steel ball about the size of a tennis ball, and hold it in your throwing hand. Then see again the picture of the confident you, again shrink it down to another steel ball and keep it with the first. Do it eight more times until you have ten steel balls in your hand; you may wish to put some of them in a pocket, in your mind.

Now you are prepared.

On a glass screen, like a TV screen or window, in your mind's eye, bring up the picture of a different you, the you that is held back by the chains, the you that you don't want to be. Now take one of those steel balls and hurl it with all your might at the glass screen containing the chained you. Watch the picture shatter with a crash, see the pieces fall to the ground, only to be blown away by the wind. And see the absolutely confident you appear from that steel ball, onto that screen. Now clear the screen.

Bring up the chained you again, on the glass screen. Take another steel ball and once more hurl it, with all your might, at the glass. See it shatter and the old you disappear and the new, confident you reappear. Keep repeating this, faster and faster, until all the balls have gone, or until you cannot bring up the chained, self-limited you again. If you can still bring up the picture, albeit by now reduced in size, colour and brightness, start again. Make some more steel balls containing the confident, positive you; try to bring up the chained picture on glass and keep throwing those steel balls, keep shattering the glass with a crash and seeing the confident you appear, until you can no longer bring the chained picture to mind.

5 *The Mirror Theory*

Just take a moment and have a conversation with yourself in the mirror and accept that you are you – there is not another person in the world who can be you. Accept this and decide to be the best you that you can be, for after all who else can be?

Rules

Rules and regulations are the boundaries within which we live our lives. 'Whose decision is it when we're offside?' 'Whose decision is it to send us off?'

Sometimes, we are just so busy and working day to day that we don't take the time to find out who set the rules of the game we're playing. It is time we took that time. We must decide on the rules for our lives, our bodies, our minds, our situations or careers, for if we don't we will live the whole of our lives by default to the rules and regulations of whoever cares to set those parameters.

'Well,' I hear you say inside your mind, 'that's a fine sentiment Peter, but what rules, what exactly do you mean?' To start with, there are some societal rules that it does make sense to obey so that the society in which we live doesn't fall into chaos or anarchy. Rules such as: you can't kill people, you must pay your taxes, you must pay for healthcare directly or indirectly, you mustn't drink and drive, you mustn't steal or commit acts of violence against people or property. These are sensible rules which form the infrastructure of the society in which we live and, yes, I am advocating we abide by them.

However, there are other rules in and of society, not passed by government, which are insidious and even restrictive and damaging to our health, happiness and potential for achievement.

There is the rule of negativity, the rule of failure, and the rules of success. Also, 'As you grow older, your memory goes with it.' 'Who do you think you are, wanting to better yourself?' 'If it was good enough for your father, it's good enough for you.' 'You better get a proper job to fall back on.' 'Don't burn your bridges.' 'Money is the root of all evil.' 'No one has ever made it from the shop floor to the board of directors in this company.' . . .

I know there have been times in my life when I have been told rules and could have agreed with them but didn't, and I'm glad I didn't. And of course there are the even more difficult ones to spot and reject, such as the peer group rules touched on earlier. 'I always feel bad on Monday morning' implies 'Don't you?' 'Thank God it's Friday, you should be pleased that the drudgery of the week is over so that you can get back to your only reason for living, Saturday night out.' (Sneeringly) 'Who does he think he is, driving a car like that, living in a house like that, wearing clothes like that?' And on and on, always implying that the speaker's opinion, the group's opinion, and – by implication, if you are going to be accepted – your opinion, must be that you accept these rules without question. Rules that say success in any form is bad, being honest is bad, being caring is bad.

This all starts at school, of course, where 'The hard-nuts' don't do their homework or don't hand it in on time, smoking behind the bikesheds or the sports pavilion, if there is one and suddenly, everyone is a follower. Following a follower, who's following a follower and, yes, it's hard to be different but it's worth every potential jibe or insult. How are we (you and I) going to break free of these negative barriers with which society and peer group pressures try to ensnare us? It really is simple, not always easy, but definitely simple.

'We need to decide our own rules.'

Yes, that's it in a nutshell: we need to decide our own rules. For example, who decided on your definition of success? I know mine used to be decided by others: TV ads, books, radios, newspapers, TV programmes, films and society at large. Unfortunately, that's a hard race to run because, every time you get near the finishing tape, somebody moves it a little bit further away. And yet it is your definition of success that really counts, your translation of that world, of that word, and all the other 'Rules' words that really matter and will make a difference to you.

Success. What is society's interpretation of the word? First, so much income per year, usually a house of a certain size, a car of a certain make, clothes with a particular label, perfume or after-shave of a particular brand, dinner at the currently fashionable restaurants, socks by 'Fred' (or whoever), shoes by 'Bill', and on and on and on.

I'm not saying these things are bad – they can be great – but only if, we consciously include them in our *own* interpretation of that most powerful seven-letter word: success.

Having lived in a big house and had extravagant cars, but also having dwelt in a flat and driven a standard car, I came to realise the trap into which I'd fallen. I'd always thought the former was my interpretation of success. Some of those things still are *my* definition, but not all of them; that's the beauty of living in a free and civilised society: we get to decide on so many of the rules. My question to you is this: 'What do you need to have, or be, or do in your life to reach your interpretation of that word success?' Are you sure you're happy, comfortable with that interpretation, or perhaps you could change it and make it easier for yourself? That's a good idea, isn't it? By changing the interpretation, you can be successful now.

So. I want you to stop and think about a new translation, a new interpretation of the success word. Here are some ideas. 'I am successful when . . . I am alive in the morning, I arrive at work, I am giving it my best shot, I smile at people I meet, I have money to spend on myself, I can look in the mirror and say, 'yes, I like you.' Or think about any monetary goals you might have, or are working towards. For example, your goal might be to be worth a certain amount of money in a certain number of years and at the moment you have just some of that amount. Well, that's success, isn't it? It is if you decide that that's your interpretation.

What about rules for other oft-used words? Take a moment to write in your definitions:

Failure
→

Accomplishment
→

Happiness
→

Wealth
→

Sadness
→

Guilt
→

Winning
→

Losing
→

More motivation

Let's look at some other ways in which our brain motivates us into action, makes us want to get up and do something and do it now. The two main feelings that create action are pain and pleasure, as already discussed. Then there is fear – Forever Expecting an Awful Result. Fear is an extremely powerful motivator, both to action and to inaction. For example, fear of the cold can make us put on warm clothes before we actually get cold.

Imagine if you were going out for a walk after lunch on a crisp, bright December day, perhaps after Christmas lunch. There's a blazing fire in the hearth, or at least the central heating is set to high. Now you know it's going to be cold outside so you put on warm clothes before you venture out. Yes, you don't wait before you get outside and catch cold, get pneumonia and lie on your deathbed to say: 'I must put on some warm clothes.' That's how fear helps us. It makes us aware that action must be taken; inaction is not the order of the day.

Fear always comes before the event; it is always more fearful before you get on stage or stand to speak than it is when you are actually performing or speaking. It is always more fearful before that sales call or meeting than it is in the meeting or call itself. So it isn't the doing that's fearful, it's the anticipation. I remember as a young man of 18 I started to play acoustic guitar and had an interest in folk music. The group I was with got a total of three unpaid gigs. The feeling of getting up before playing was fear personified; dry mouth, damp hands, queasy stomach – the works; but once on stage and into the music it was great. In fact, after the third song I was actually enjoying myself and was disappointed it all had to finish. To repeat: the fear was in the anticipation, not in the doing; in fact, the perceived pain of refusing to go on and letting down the other members of the group and perhaps, most importantly, myself, was a greater pain than having to go on stage.

In other words, the lesser pain was the way, the greater pain was definitely not the way. Knowing that fear is in the anticipation not the realisation can be a great help to us. For we get the opportunity to think about the upcoming situation, and therefore Face the fear, Evaluate the fear, Analyse the fear and Reject the fear; FEAR. And this is how we can deal with fear in every area of our lives.

Obviously, emergency situations which engender fear need immediate action. The feeling of potentially being hit by a falling tree requires an instant response: run!

The feeling associated with accomplishments, achievements, success, meetings and speaking can be overcome. First, write down on a piece of paper a question or questions to yourself. For example:

1 What do I want as the outcome of this situation? Be as specific as you can
2 Why do I want this outcome? Motivate yourself with pain and gain; remember the seesaw? We need stacks of reasons why we must take action. Use the pain of your relationship with those you love and respect and your relationship with yourself. For example, you have an upcoming event, social or commercial, when you know you will have to stand and speak, and the thought of it produces a variety of feelings. Maybe some of those feelings are negative, including fear in some of its forms – of criticism, failure, rejection, success, ridicule, embarrassment, or of such bodily discomfitures as blushing or knees knocking. 'I might be judged!' Fear of a low opinion of self, fear of a low opinion of your own worth . . . Fear.

   So first write out the outcome, the results you want. It might be to persuade the Parent Teachers Association to your point of view, to convince the Board of Directors that your raise is due – and due now – to thank a group of visitors for attending a social function, so they leave happier with the day. Write out why you want it, using pleasure. Then write out why you want it, using pain.
3 Decide on your own rules.
4 Write out the best possible outcome.
5 Write out the worst possible outcome.

6 Write out your opinion of the likely outcome.
7 Say out loud, 'I have decided to . . .'
8 Enjoy the nerves, it's only adrenaline. It lets you know you're alive and not a robot.
9 Use Self-talk to reprogramme the computer between your ears.
10 Fake it 'til you make it.

By the time you have reached this point, then you will be wanting to take action now. If it is possible, do it now; if not, take a note of how you are feeling, standing, breathing, look in the mirror and remember what you look like so that you can recall this image. Have you got your fists clenched, are you saying, 'Yes, I can do it'?

Remember what that switch is. Now that decision is made, you can do it – even better, you'll know why you're going to do it and the rewards of that accomplishment. So, here are the steps:

1 List the chains that have been holding you back.
2 Forgive those who imposed the chains.
3 Decide which method you will use to break the chains:
   - By being aware of the chain, meaning that it will no longer affect you.
   - The Eyes of Love and Understanding.
   - Reprogramming the In-talk.
   - Burning the Bridges.
   - The Shatter Principle.
4 List the areas of your life (see also the Time Management section).
5 Think of what rules you are living by, in those areas.
6 Decide and write down the rules by which you will live.
7 List any fears you may have.
8 Decide to keep the ones that help you.
9 Go through the process we covered to get rid of the ones you want to lose.
10 Find and remember the switch that you know will rocket you past your fear.

If you have beliefs that empower you, if you set the rules for your life, if you welcome and deal with fear in the way in which I have described, then you can accomplish anything – if you take enthusiastic action.

2 Make It Happen

Summary. Throughout this chapter, we are going to be talking about taking action, about how to take the right actions to get the results that you want in your life. Then we will look at making decisions, including a decision-making test, and list ten different ways of making effective decisions. Finally, we will discuss dealing with other people, how to get them to take action, and how to improve our relationships in all our interactions with others.

Taking action

In the previous chapter we started to interpret our own translation for the words success, failure, happiness, sadness and, or course, accomplishment. We now need to take a moment to redefine, re-translate and re-interpret those words – and many others – to ensure that we are constantly living by our own rules. In this taking action session, we are going to be looking at where we are now, where we want to be, how to do visualisations (often talked about but seldom explained), a new way to start conversations, and the 22 or so reasons that people use in order to avoid making important decisions.

Then we will look at conditioned responses and a circuit-breaker technique to remove negativity in ourselves and others; how to create the personal attitudes we want to have and how to erase old habits by using four different methods; and finally, how to create a switch for yourself to enable you to experience any feeling you want, at any time you want it.

The benefits of all this will be that you'll be better at making decisions, you'll know how to work out the actions you need to take to accomplish what you want, and you will have a positive impact on all your dealings with others – with the obvious results that that brings. You'll be using more of your current skills, you'll be able to erase old negative patterns and beliefs and implant the positive patterns that you have decided you want in your life. I also believe that, by the end of this section, you will be more optimistic, more enthusiastic and more self-motivated to do the things you want to do in your life, simply to accomplish more.

The six-stage process. Throughout my life, I have used a six-stage process in order to help me take action:

1. Where are you now?
2. How did you get here?
3. Where are you going?
4. Why do you want to go there?
5. What are the possible obstacles?
6. What are you going to do?

Self

'Where am I now?'

'How did I get here?'

'Where am I going?'

'Why do I want to go there?'

'What are the possible obstacles?'

'What am I going to do?'

Family

'Where am I now?'

'How did I get here?'

'Where am I going?'

'Why do I want to go there?'

'What are the possible obstacles?'

'What am I going to do?'

Friends

'Where am I now?'

'How did I get here?'

'Where am I going?'

'Why do I want to go there?'

'What are the possible obstacles?'

'What am I going to do?'

Financial matters

'Where am I now?'

'How did I get here?'

'Where am I going?'

'Why do I want to go there?'

'What are the possible obstacles?'

'What am I going to do?'

Career

'Where am I now?'

'How did I get here?'

'Where am I going?'

'Why do I want to go there?'

'What are the possible obstacles?'

'What am I going to do?'

Learning/Self development

'Where am I now?'

'How did I get here?'

'Where am I going?'

'Why do I want to go there?'

'What are the possible obstacles?'

'What am I going to do?'

Spiritual matters

'Where am I now?'

'How did I get here?'

'Where am I going?'

'Why do I want to go there?'

'What are the possible obstacles?'

'What am I going to do?'

Relationships

'Where am I now?'

'How did I get here?'

'Where am I going?'

'Why do I want to go there?'

'What are the possible obstacles?'

'What am I going to do?'

Emotions

'Where am I now?'

'How did I get here?'

'Where am I going?'

'Why do I want to go there?'

'What are the possible obstacles?'

'What am I going to do?'

Accomplishments

'Where am I now?'

'How did I get here?'

'Where am I going?'

'Why do I want to go there?'

'What are the possible obstacles?'

'What am I going to do?'

Social

'Where am I now?'

'How did I get here?'

'Where am I going?'

'Why do I want to go there?'

'What are the possible obstacles?'

'What am I going to do?'

Health

'Where am I now?'

'How did I get here?'

'Where am I going?'

'Why do I want to go there?'

'What are the possible obstacles?'

'What am I going to do?'

Physical

'Where am I now?'

'How did I get here?'

'Where am I going?'

'Why do I want to go there?'

'What are the possible obstacles?'

'What am I going to do?'

Self-esteem

'Where am I now?'

'How did I get here?'

'Where am I going?'

'Why do I want to go there?'

'What are the possible obstacles?'

'What am I going to do?'

One of the things that sometimes stopped me from accomplishing things I wanted in life was a chain my mother had inadvertently, and for the best reasons, put on me. She would often say, 'Moderation in all things', and I know what she meant: she meant enjoy yourself but be home in time; by all means enjoy a drink but don't drink too much; by all means enjoy good food but don't each so much that you cannot walk.

The problem with chains is that they have a habit of forming themselves into areas and onto areas which weren't originally intended for them. One of my mottos became: 'Moderation in all things'. This prevented me from taking the amount of enthusiastic action which was necessary to accomplish some of my dreams. When I realised I was carrying this chain it was easy to break; I knew I had to give it 100% to get the plane to fly – and then, and only then, could I ease back on the throttle. Could some of the reasons for not accomplishing some of the things you wanted to, in the areas we have just explored, be because of chains? Could it simply be that your interpretation of some words like success, failure and accomplishment were other people's definitions?

Fear often comes into play. Scientists say that when we were children, the only two fears we had were those of falling and loud noises. Although 'falling' is one that's sometimes hard to understand for parents, if you know of children, like mine, who may seen to be budding mountaineers, ready to tackle the North Face of the Eiger, that is to say the back of the settee or the steps of the bunk-beds, at such an early age.

When we were young, we didn't have the so-called 'adult fears', the fear of embarrassment. You could be attending a social function, perhaps a wedding reception or a large party, be quite prepared to be the first on the dance floor, happy to show off your new clothes, and squeal with delight, 'Mum, Dad, look at me!' – or wander round the beach with no clothes on, oblivious to the stares. As we grow up we learn, and that's the important word, we learn the fear of embarrassment.

Failure. This is my least favourite word, another of those adult words allied to fear of success, fear of heights, fear of fire, fear of flying, fear of the opposite sex; all these fears, these preventers of action, that we learn from others – we must break through, we must keep on breaking these chains. A number of methods to achieve this were described in the previous chapter, and they can be used to good effect. The major way is by In-talk Out-talk programming. Let's look again, at In-talk at In-look, at In-feel, and at an oft-used word – visualisation.

Visualisation

Many people struggle with visualisation and I have, in the past. I always though that everyone was seeing a full 'Cinemascope' film running in their minds, full colour, full sounds, 'Dolby Stereo' and the like, and that I was the only one struggling with no picture or a black and white dim picture at best, fuzzy sound – a general feeling of disappointment at what was happening. If this has happened to you when you try to visualise, then I know the following will help.

First, visualisation is a word which seems to indicate that you should see pictures. Well, they are not absolutely necessary. It is more than sufficient to *feel* the pictures. If, in your mind's eye, you can vividly feel the pictures or intensely feel the emotion, that's great; or if you can't see the pictures or experience the feelings, simply try to see or hear or even feel the words. Each person has his or her own way of visualising and it is only the 'visual' word that makes everyone think it must be pictures. Not so. It's whatever works for you.

If you haven't done any conscious visualisations, don't necessarily expect to see the full-colour movie immediately. Accept whatever happens for you; it's OK. If you want to see pictures, actual pictures, it usually takes practice. Here are some ways to do it:

1 Look at a scene, any scene, for a second or two, then close your eyes and try to conjure up the scene in your mind. Now open your eyes again and look at the scene for a further one or two seconds. Then close your eyes again and try once more to conjure up the scene. Keep on doing this: one or two seconds of looking and one or two of visualising. Practice of this type will enhance your ability to see pictures – if that's what you want.
2 Sit comfortably in a chair, with your head upright and your back straight – erect but not stiff. Now, with your eyes closed, look up from the horizontal plane to about 20 or 25 degrees above the horizontal. Let me explain that again: with your head erect, but not stiff, with your eyes closed, imagine that your are looking straight out in front of you. Now move your eyes to look slightly upwards, higher than before. Imagine, if you can, that you are looking at a screen or TV placed about 10 feet away from you, but keep your eyes closed.

This looking-up method can work well – it is the one I use and often I imagine that the screen is the screen of my computer, and as I use Windows I can ask the computer to bring up any pictures I want. It all takes practice.

If you want to find out whether pictures, feelings, words or sounds are the ones for you, ask yourself the following questions:

'Can you see yourself on a beach?' If you can see yourself, then you are probably visualising in pictures, if the answer is 'no', then:

'Can you feel yourself on a beach?' If the answer is 'yes', you can probably visualise in feelings, if the answer is still 'no':

'Can you hear yourself on a beach, or hear the word "beach" in you mind?' If the answer is 'yes', then you are probably visualising in words or sounds.

This is all part of the Subconscious Encoding Process described in Chapter 1. The problem for some people is simply that their language is visually based, incorporating such words as 'scene', 'visualising', 'imagining' and 'imagine' (looking at the pictures, the images, in our minds), so that they believe visualising has to be pictures or nothing. No. I repeat: it's whatever works best for you.

We know that our actions come from our thoughts, so I now want you to try some 'thought to action processes'.

Thought to action processes

Sit up or stand up as straight as you can, feel positive, have a positive attitude, feel confident, feel that you are a 'can do' person, nothing can stop you from accomplishing anything you want. Doesn't that feel great?

Now take enthusiastic action, make a note of the look, the talk, the feelings.

Now go to the other end and say negative things about yourself: 'I'm no good, I can't do it, I'm too old, I'm too young, I simply can't accomplish anything.' Make a mental note of what is happening: your posture, your feelings, your language, your face, your breathing. OK, you don't want to stay at that end, so let's have a few positives to get back on track: 'I am a "can do" person, I like myself, I'm happy with me.'

Now it's decision time again. At which end of the scale are you going to live your life? Decide now, get that In-talk, In-look, In-feel programme working *for* you, not against you. Walk and talk and act the way you want to act, decide to act, start talking like the person you want to be, start doing the things, taking the actions, that that person would take, that you want to be.

'Just fake it 'til you make it'

You can't save up your energy, so let's start using it. When you meet someone and they ask 'How are you?', what do you say? I have found that over 90% of the world says 'Fine'. However, there are a variety of ways of saying this four-letter word: it could be 'Fine' (slowly), 'Fine' (sharply), or 'Fine' (loudly). Unless we are using it about the weather, I hate the word. I think that it could as well stand for Feeling Inwardly Negative Everyday, and I have a one-man crusade to end its use in response to 'How are you?'

What I'd like you to do is to find a new way of responding to this perennial question. You could say 'Tremendous' or 'Great' or 'Fantastic' – that's not to say you have to go right over the top, but a response of this kind is a way of starting all conversations on a positive note. You will be surprised at the difference it will make.

I share this idea on the seminars I run, whether they are in-house seminars or open seminars, and it's great to see everyone trying to catch each other out during the day by saying 'Fine'.

Some years ago I ran an in-house personal development and sales seminar for an American company which had a UK operation in Southampton. They'd flown in the managing directors of their German and Dutch operations for the course and after I had explained my views about the word 'Fine', I asked everyone to think of a new response. The Dutch director, who spoke exceptionally good English, said that in future he would respond with, 'I am like a tiger'. You can imagine the hilarity that caused, and for the rest of the two-day course everyone was responding likewise – so much so that it has now caught on as an in-company joke. Fun? Yes, but with a serious intent.

If we start our conversation with everybody with whom we interact on a positive 'can do' note, the ensuing conversation often continues in that positive mode. I know people who say 'Top of the world' or 'Really fabulous' or all sorts of things, and have been amazed at the difference that such a simple thing can make to any atmosphere or situation. Try it for yourself and see what happens (I use 'Tremendous' or 'Stunning'). It has now got to the stage where people phone me and don't ask how I am, they *tell* me. They say: 'I suppose you are as tremendous as always.' What better start to any conversation, particularly with clients and customers?

Like any habit it will take time for you to become accustomed, and from time to time you may find yourself saying 'Fine' and have to 'retune your strings' to the new expression that you have decide upon.

We're talking about taking action and we can be helped in this by the goal-setting exercise that comes later and by the affirmations we examined earlier. Confidence, I always feel, is in the application of confidence: if we do something that requires confidence we become confident; and if we become confident, we do confident things – it just goes round and round. So, let the new you be more confident, act confidently, speak confidently – and you will become confident. The beauty of that is that like attracts like. When you act positive, happy and confident, you will find that you attract positive, happy and confident people into your life and that others around you become happier, more confident and more positive.

'You can't fly with the eagles if you work with the turkeys.'

We all take actions in direct relationship to the pictures, the feelings and the words we use to describe ourselves – this is called the self-concept. If we use the principle of anticipation – anticipating things will always get the results we require, anticipating that we are positive – then we will be confident that we will be positive.

Some years ago I was at a parents' 'do' at the school of my eldest son – he was in the school scouts and they were having a barbecue for the parents and demonstrating some of the skills they had learned. During the course of the evening, I met a man I had previously met some years before; he was the assistant manager of a small branch of one of the UK's major banks. He was, I'm sorry to say, somewhat of a negative character. A small boy, one of the younger scouts who had been delegated to sell the raffle tickets, approached the banker and asked him, in somewhat tentative terms, if he would be prepared to buy any raffle tickets. The man's response: 'Well, I suppose so, though why I'm bothering I don't know, I never win anything at raffles.'

The boy approached me, again with the same tentative request, 'Er, excuse me sir, would you like to buy any raffle tickets?' 'Of course,' I replied, 'I always buy raffle tickets because I always win prizes at raffles.'

The draw was made. There was only one prize – one of those large glasses of sweets, with a black plastic screw-on top, that used to be in the sweet-shops when we were children – and the winning ticket? In my hand. I don't know why these things work or how they work, I only know they do.

It's as though the world always gives to those who believe the world will give, it's as though it sets up the situation in your favour, just like parking the car. It also appears that the reverse is true; if you expect that the world won't favour you, won't give you what you want, that you won't be able to park . . . that's exactly what you get. Who knows why it works? It just does. If we can be enthusiastic in our dealings with people, they become enthusiastic – again, this is not to say that you go over-the-top and people run away. Enthusiasm is an extremely contagious condition. I used to think it the most contagious condition known to man, but I was wrong; *lack* of enthusiasm is the most contagious disease. See a motivational speech to a team of people, having everyone fired up and ready to go and one member of the team, on the way out, says, 'Er, the usual old stuff, I don't believe I can do it', and watch the other members of the team all sink at the same time. Let's make sure that we are not in that category.

If you have to speak at your place of work, or any social engagement, and the purpose of your talk is motivation, before you finish speaking make sure that no one else wants to say anything, so that the last words heard by the audience are your call to action. Having ignored this advice, to my cost, on more than one occasion, I have learned by the results . . . be the last to speak.

So let's talk more about taking action. We know that action produces results, that knowledge is wasted if we don't use it. It is no good being able to see if we don't look. It is no good being able to read if we don't read. It is no good being able to hear if we don't listen. It's the same with all of our commercial and social skills. As I have said before, how many people do you know who never achieve the level of success that their level of skill says they should? Could one of those people be you? Are you at the level that your level of skill says you should be at? If not, why?

Maybe you are not using your skills often enough, only *you* know. Sometimes we meet people who say they have ten, 20 or even 30 years' experience in their chosen field. Sometimes they have only one year's experience, ten, 20 or 30 times. They still keep doing what they always did, they still keep getting what they always got, and the crying shame is that they are often surprised that their results haven't changed. Let's examine the reasons why people don't take action:

1 Poor self-management.
2 Lack of motivation.
3 Held back by chains.
4 Fear.
5 Doing what they always did.
6 Living by the rules imposed by others.
7 No definition of success.
8 No knowledge of what actions to take.
9 Poor dealings with other people.
10 Dishonesty with self and others.
11 Poor time management.
12 No goals set.
13 Lack of understanding about brain – and mind-learning skills and motivation.
14 No use of creative skills.
15 Stress through lack of planning.
16 No financial planning.
17 Poor use of communication skills.
18 No persistency and no consistency.
19 Fear of risk-taking.
20 Fear of failure.
21 Perfectionism.

And of course the big one: *no decision made to take action.*

All of these reasons for lack of action, we have covered, or will cover, throughout the course of this book. So, let's look now at making decisions.

Making decisions

Imagine the situation: you're lying in bed, it's a cold morning, the heating has broken down, you're warm in bed but the room is freezing. Now, physically getting out of bed is easy; one leg out, two legs out, stand up and away you go. Actually making the decision to get out of bed . . . that's the hard part. And that's so often the way with so many things in our lives; doing them is easy, deciding to do them is the hard part. You'll know situations like this yourself; you'd been putting off something, and then for some reason or other you decided to take action. As soon as the decision was made, taking action was easy – and yes, we are all making decisions all day long, many of them are unconscious decisions; when to sleep, when to eat, when to play, when to work – unconscious decisions and in many ways habit decisions. That word habit is the key; there are so many habits we have; the habitual way we cross our arms, interlock our fingers, dress ourselves, lace our shoes – so many little habits taking place every single day. Here's something to try: try changing some of those small habits – just small ones to start with, so that you are living your life less by default to habits and more in control, with a sense of knowing which habits are affecting your actions. You might tie your shoes in a different order, you might practise crossing your arms or interlocking your fingers in a different way. To start with it will seem awkward, but after a time you get a new habit, a habit that says you're making conscious actions.

This practice at making decisions is a great help to get you started, in order to create the . . . habit . . . of making major decisions. Let's do one now – make a decision, something small, not something that's going to change the world, something perhaps you've been putting off, just *decide* that you will do it.

OK? Decided? Wasn't that easy? Now here is a decision-making test:

Above are four cards. The cards are printed as follows:

Every card which has a vowel on the front always has an even number on the back. The question I want to ask you is: 'Which card or cards do you need to turn over in order to prove that the above statement is not untrue?'
Please decide on which card or cards you would turn over before looking at the answer on the next page.

The answer is E and 3.

Now that you have attempted this decision-making test, let's examine why many people are unable to get it right. We need to turn over the E card to find out if a vowel is on the back. Most people get that right; however, we also need to turn over the 3 card, because we need to know if there is a vowel on the back of it, too. If there is a vowel on the back of it, then the statement is untrue. If there is a consonant, then the statement is true – provided there's an even number on the back of the E card.

What does all this mean and how does it help in making good decisions?

Usually, most people ask what's called 'confirming questions' and not what are called 'opposing questions'. In the above test, the confirming question was: 'Is there an even number on the back of the E card?' The opposing question was: 'Is there a vowel on the back of the 3 card?'

This is so useful in many different situations. In many interviews, candidates for a position are asked only about things which confirm that they can do the job. But it is also essential to ask questions which may lead to information which proves that they cannot do the job.

When trying to decide which actions to take, it is useful to ask yourself questions which look at all possibilities for action and all possibilities for non-action. Questions such as 'What do I know which proves that something is right?' and 'What do I know which proves that something is wrong?' are extremely useful in making good-quality decisions.

If I had taken this test many years ago, I am certain that some of the decisions I made in life which subsequently proved costly in time, money or effort would not have been made. Making decisions, or the lack of making decisions, can sometimes come down to the lack of planning. I like to think of planning as a four-step process, as the diagram overleaf illustrates:

It's a very simple process. You set your goals, the goals indicate the plan, the plan indicates the actions you must take, the actions taken produce feedback, the feedback enables us to check that we still want that particular goal, and back through the system. Constantly taking action, checking the feedback (feedback from the outside world and feedback from our own thoughts and feelings) and checking the goals and planning; very simple to produce, very simple to operate.

It's often been said that many people plan their wedding ceremonies more carefully than they plan their marriages. Many people plan their holidays better than they plan their lives – and yet . . . planning is essential. Proper Planning Prevents Particularly Poor Performance: the Six Ps Principle.

Planning ensures that we are taking the right actions, the actions we've planned to take, the actions we have decided upon in response to our decision-making question: 'What do I need to do to . . .' The actions produce only feedback . . . no failures, only results, from which we can check the goals and the plan.

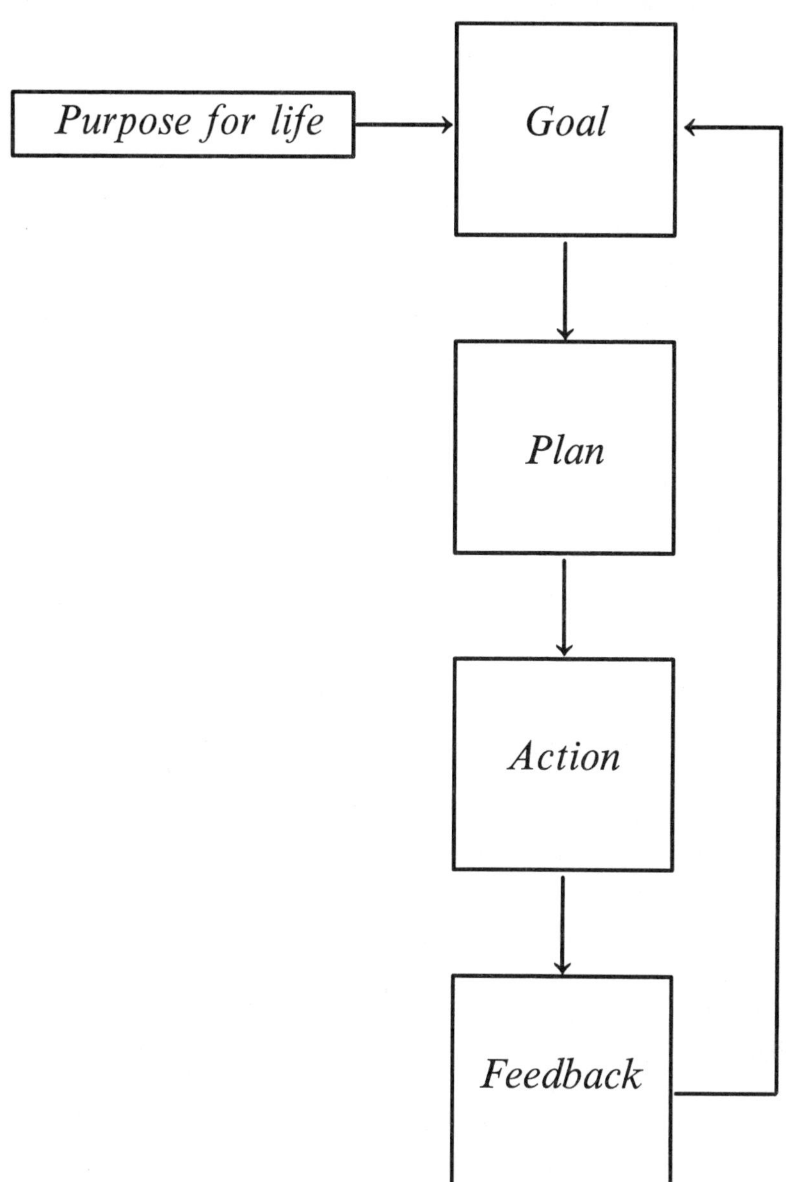
Purpose for life
Goal
Plan
Action
Feedback

'Mistakes are only evidence that someone tried to do something.'

The Maradonna Principle. One of the principles I use in order to keep my attitude positive is called 'The Maradonna Principle'. It is named after the famous Argentinian soccer player, Diego Maradonna – and it's not to do with the 'Hand of God' World Cup incident. I'm thinking of the time that Maradonna was considered to be the best soccer player in the world. What usually happened to Maradonna, almost every time he had possession of the ball in the opponent's half of the pitch, was that he was tripped, often elbowed or fouled. He was tripped over so often that it seems he almost spent half of his playing time lying on the pitch. Why? Simply because he was trying to score. No one ever tripped up a soccer player when he wasn't a threat to anyone, threatening to score, threatening to pass the ball to someone else who was likely to score. The only time you get tripped up is when you are trying to score – and that's what life does as well: it sometimes tries to trip us up, but only when we're trying to score.

Now, as always, we have a choice. We can play in the middle of the park and try and score, or we can play on the sidelines as the judge, linesman or referee. On the line we won't get tripped, we won't get elbowed and we won't get fouled – but neither will we score.

If we have decide to play, we must also accept that with that territory come the knocks, the fouls, the trip-ups when we are trying to score. Who tries to trip us up? It might be the competition; the other teams playing our game, the other suppliers of the type of products our company sells or produces. It might be our colleagues or the company, it might even be the income tax department – or perhaps, at times, even ourselves.

Let's accept it, let's be aware that it will happen only when we are nearing our goal. Let's look on it as feedback that the world is giving us that we must be close, and so, when those occasions come along, don't just lie there, get up and keep going, for you must be so close.

The large block of granite in the path of a weak person is treated as a stumbling block, but in the path of a strong person, with the right attitude, it becomes a stepping stone to higher and better things. That is the attitude anyone must have if they are going to accomplish anything.

I mentioned in my short story, The life and times of Peter Thomson, the problems I had with shares that lost nine-tenths of their value – nearly three million pounds, and that's a lot to lose. However, there is one silver lining to that cloud; you have to have three million in order to lose three million – and as there are no failures, just lessons to be learned, I learned some hard lessons. In life, some lessons are easy lessons and some are hard, but they are all only results if we have the right attitude.

Getting up and taking action, enthusiastic action, is the key. It is the cause that creates an effect, which begins a new road, which creates a destination, which helps us reach our goals and the accomplishments we want.

When I am talking to people at sales seminars about why people buy, we discuss a number of areas. One is obviously that people buy benefits and not simply features, and we have already used this idea in selling ourselves on ourselves, focusing on what we will accomplish by taking action, the principle of the see-saw.

The other area we cover at those seminars is this: I ask people to remember the last three times that someone tried to sell something to them, maybe at home, at work or even in a shop, and they didn't buy. I ask them to list the reasons why they didn't buy. The biggest factor in their decision not to buy, in the great majority of cases, is the salesperson who is trying to sell the product or service. Then, to salespeople: 'Think of the last three times you tried to make a sale and didn't succeed, and list the reasons why you think the sale didn't go ahead, didn't reach a successful conclusion.' The reasons are as varied as they are illuminating: the buyer was a pig, the buyer wouldn't listen to reason, our price was too high – and it always is – our product simply doesn't compete in our marketplace, our delivery is useless, our credit policy is so old it was designed by Adam and Eve, and so on.

The only factor that always seems to be missing is the salesperson themselves. Why is it, when we are buying, that the salesperson is one of the prime factors in our decision, but when were selling it makes no difference? Why indeed . . .

It is the same with anybody when there are actions to be taken: the difference in any situation regarding you . . . is you. How did you sell yourself on being where you are now, how will you – and it must be you – sell yourself on where you want to be, or what you want to accomplish?

Conditioning. You've heard of the Russian scientist Ivan Pavlov, the Nobel Prize winner who experimented with dogs. Pavlov gave his dogs food and at the same time rang a bell, sounded a tone. The dogs became conditioned to the sound and salivated when they heard the bell or tone. The dogs had learned a conditioned response to a conditioned stimulus. (Sidenote: the original Russian word, in fact, meant 'conditional' not 'conditioned' but usage has changed the expression to conditioned.) With this method, Pavlov defined learning as a behavioural change produced by biological conditioning, and of course we all have these conditioned responses. We have them for all our senses. We hear a certain piece of music and it evokes certain memories; people often say, 'Oh, that's our tune' to a particular melody for this reason. We have conditioned responses to things we see, things we touch. The certain feel of a certain object will again create a certain response. Certain smells will bring back memories, the smell of bread, the sea or the old-fashioned steam-engine smoke has us re-living past experiences in our mind. The taste of certain food or drinks can bring memories of holidays from years ago.

So how can we use this knowledge? First, we can create for ourselves a negative habit circuit-breaker. When you find yourself saying or thinking something negative, have a penalty. For example, in one of my companies, when someone said something negative, not realistic, mind you (realism was OK), but negative, they had to do ten press-ups. Negativity was quickly erased. You can decide on some minor penalty for yourself to create that circuit-breaker; you might pinch yourself, not have that cup of coffee, jump up and down on the spot for two minutes, whatever – just something that will probably make you smile and have others around you thinking you've probably gone quite mad. Use it, it really does work.

Then there's the Shatter Method (see Chapter 1), and the Switch Method. This is how to use it; feel the feeling you want, remember, you've already used this idea to get positive by saying positive things, acting positively, getting into that state of mind and body. Now, when you are feeling really positive, create a switch, like a lightswitch – it could be a clenched fist, a pinch on the arm, a spot on the back of your hand that you press with the forefinger of your other hand, standing on one leg, it can be anything you choose.

Get into the state of mind and body to make the switch; then do it again and again and again, keep pressing the switch. Now you have created a conditioned response to a conditioned stimulus. When you press the switch, you will instantly go into the state of mind and body to the link of that switch. Practise with this. As with all of these ideas, it has been tried and tested and proven to work for other people, and I know it will work for you.

Visualisation, as already explained, can be whatever you determine it to be: pictures, feelings or sounds. If you are into sounds, then play an audio tape in your head of you doing the thing you want to erase; then, as the audio tape is playing, superimpose the sounds of you being the way you want to be. Keep playing the tape until you can't hear you . . . in the old way.

If you are a visual visualiser, then do the same but with a video tape. Imagine that the picture of you which you want to erase is playing but on the TV in your mind, and in the corner of that picture is another small screen, rather like the 'picture within a picture' facility on TV videos. While the video is playing, have that small picture in the corner, that picture of how you want to be . . . watch it get larger and larger and larger until it takes over the whole picture and erases the old you. Keep playing the tape until the new you takes over and until you cannot bring up the old picture of you.

If you are a feelings person, all of your visualisations are feelings, use both of the methods just described. They will work.

The Steps

1 Take time to discover the actions you have taken that have brought you to this stage in your life.
2 Reprogramme your In-talk on the basis that you are a 'can do' person, who does take action.
3 Decide, for definite, on the new way that you will respond to 'How are you?'
4 Make another decision now . . . an easy one. Get into the habit of making decisions.
5 Change the easy habits.
6 List your skills.
7 Find out why, if appropriate, from the list of 21 reasons for non-action, you may not yet have reached the level of success or accomplishment that your level of skill says you should have reached.
8 Decide to use your skills to the full and be open to learning new skills on a regular basis.

'The day we stop learning is the day we stop earning.'

9 Decide to use written self-questions as one of your major self-management tools.
10 Try each of the decision-making ideas at least once to find out which one works best for you.
11 Decide on a negative circuit-breaker.
12 Use the Switch Method we have just discussed to create your own conditioned response.
13 Destroy those action-preventing beliefs by spoiling the tapes and with the Shatter Method.

I know we have covered a massive amount of information, ideas and techniques in this section and it is going to take time to work through everything. However, the long road to accomplishment starts with just one step and that step is your decision to take . . . enthusiastic action.

Dealing with others

This section, then, is all about dealing with other people, all the other people in your life. Why people like you and respect you; more about self-management and making the changes to improve your relationships with others. Briefly, dealing with children, dealing with partners, looking at the attributes of the people you mix with socially and commercially, learning from other people, how we are influenced by those around us. Some basics of leadership and understanding, why a work team does what it does. Some of the 'how to's' in interactions with others, criticism and how to criticise (if criticise we must), The Boomerang Principle and its effect on us, all in all . . . people.

The benefits you will gain will be a better understanding of why people do what they do and some simple, tried and tested methods to get more out of your relationships with people . . . *all* the people in your life. All of our accomplishments in life are related to people, either as a direct interaction with them, or by utilising the objects that they have made for us. Just look around where you are now: did you make most of the things you can see? Probably not – I know I didn't. I wouldn't have the first idea how to make a computer, or even a pen for that matter. Perhaps, together, we could make a desk, but it probably wouldn't be as good as one of the desks that we could buy from a shop. So, if we are in a position in life where we have to deal with people, and it's really only hermits on desert islands who don't, it would be as well to understand people as much as possible. One of the best ways to deal with anyone in life is to have esteem for them. So try and build self-esteem in other people by sincerely complimenting them on the actions they take. This mustn't be flattery or a technique, for if it's false, it will be seen through every time. You have probably experienced false praise at some time in your life and I am certain it would have sent a shudder down your back and reduced your like or respect for the person concerned.

However, if you can find reasons, honest reasons, to compliment a person on their actions, if you can find honest reasons to build the self-esteem of others, then whatever you have said to them to produce that effect will be words and efforts well used. When giving compliments, make sure that you compliment the action not the person. Compliments aimed direct to the person can sound 'sugary' or sycophantic, whereas compliments aimed at the actions that people have taken are far more acceptable.

For example, imagine a salesperson has been accompanied by the sales manager into an important call, which turned out successfully; a completed sale. The *wrong way* would be: 'Do you know boss, when you come with me to the calls, it's as though you're a bright light shining on me and the customer, you're the number one as far as I'm concerned!' That would have most people reaching for the door handle, or worse. However, the *right way* would be: 'John, I really appreciate your help in that call, particularly when you were able to answer that technical question. Thanks!' That would have a far better effect. Let me again stress: compliments must be honest.

'Be interested . . . not interesting.'

We discussed earlier that everyone has their role to play and that, usually, they are the best judge of what is the best course of action. Trying to convince someone to go along your road may be a good idea; however, if they are determined to follow their own path, support them. They will respect you for it and return your support. For people to like you, you have to like people; life is a mirror and there is usually something to like in most people. We can, at a superficial level, like the way they look, like the way they dress, we might like their opinions; but we like people whose opinions match our own. We can find something to like about most people, even if we have to dig to find it.

We like people who like us, in exactly the same way as people like us if we like them. The same goes for interest, pride and respect: if you can respect another person, chances are the respect will be reciprocated. If you can be proud of another person or their efforts or accomplishments, no doubt they will be proud of you and yours. If you can be genuinely interested in other people, they will have a greater interest in you. Life really is a mirror.

We know that the only way to accomplish anything we want is to be the boss of Me Unlimited. If we have people around us, people in our teams, both socially and commercially, we have to *lead* them and not manage them. We have to teach them, if it's appropriate, the skills of self-management.

One of the ways we can improve our dealings with others is to be able to see ourselves and our actions through the eyes of others; for example:

1 How would your parents describe you?
   Have you turned out according to their expectations, or have you perhaps travelled your own road? Whichever – did they respect and support you in those adventures?
2 If you have children, how would they describe you? Are you the ideal role model for them? Are they proud that you are their parent?
3 How would your boss describe you?
4 How would your employees describe you?
5 How would your friends describe you?
6 How would your suppliers describe you?
7 How would your customers describe you?
8 If you're in sales, how would your buyers describe you?
9 If you're in buying, how would the salespeople describe you?
10 How would your work colleagues describe you?
11 How would your partner describe you?

If you are able, for a moment, to think what others might think about you, it really can be the most useful exercise. It lets you know if the actions you're taking in relation to those other people in your life are having the effect, the results, you would wish for.

If you were your parent, child, boss, employee, friend, supplier, buyer, seller, customer, colleague, partner, how would you, in their position, answer these four questions about you?

1 What do you like about this person?
2 What do you dislike about this person?
3 What skills, attributes and attitudes would you keep in this person?

4 What skills, attributes and attitudes would you change in this person?

All of these self-questioning techniques are the basis of self-management. As already said, we usually have most of the skills we need. We usually have most of the answers to life's questions. We just need to access the information, and the easiest way in the world is to ask yourself questions, letting your brain supply the answers.

My suggestion is this: when you have an opportunity, go through that list of people again, the full list, and write down the four questions – and answer them. That is self-management in relationship to others.

Dealing with children. We know that our parents probably put chains on us, creating, for all the best reasons, limiting beliefs. As the sergeant in TV's *Hill Street Blues* always used to say: 'Let's be careful out there!' Let's be careful what we are saying to children. 'You'll never amount to anything!', said by a parent or a teacher, can have a devastating effect on a child. Why? Because the child believes it. Whatever you say to a child, particularly a small child, as a parent or someone else in authority, that child will believe. Let's make sure that we are teaching children to be 'can do' people, prepared to tread their own path in life. Teach them the skills, expect the best from them, and they will probably give you their best.

Have you noticed that if you say to children 'Be careful, don't drop that plate', they often do drop the plate? Or 'Don't walk too close to the edge, you'll fall'. And of course they do fall. It is because of the way our brain copes with negatives; the Subconscious Encoding Process again.

When you tell children 'Don't drop the plate', or 'Don't walk too close to the edge, you'll fall', the instruction they get is 'Drop the plate – don't', or 'Fall off – don't'. They are difficult commands with which to comply; far better to say 'Hold the plate tightly' or 'Walk a little further in' or 'Hold on firmly to the rungs of the ladder when you are climbing'. All of these are positive commands and helpful suggestions. If you listen to the language used with children, you'll find much of it, unfortunately, is phrased in the negative. You can have some fun with this insight, sharing it with others, and making a game whose object is to catch others' negatives and change them into positives.

Dealing with partners. Let's now look at our partners and spouses. We know that incoming love and outgoing love are major psychological needs. And it's great to have a loving relationship with another human being. Liking is important too; if you *love* someone, but don't *like* them, or the actions they take, then you have problems. Find *something* to like. We will deal with criticism shortly.

One of the killers of marriages and relationships can be jealousy and this comes from a lack of trust. If we do things to create worry or a lack of trust in our partner, is it any wonder that jealousy will surface? Jealousy is the effect, no trust is the cause. To have a happy marriage, do that most difficult thing we ever have to do . . . decide! Make a decision to have a happy marriage, use the decision-making methods. On a piece a paper, write a question to yourself which would go like this: 'What do I need to do, be or have to have a happy marriage?' Get your partner to do the same, but do it separately and then compare notes. Keep the compatible ideas and discuss and resolve the incompatible ones. Sounds too simple? Yes . . . it is, but how many people have taken the time to plan their marriages? It's back to the Six P's Principle: Proper Planning Prevents Particularly Poor Performance.

An area that is definitely worthy of discussion is how you and your partner get the opportunity to be just yourselves – psychological need for privacy, for time for the self. So often situations can arise where people are always somebody else's 'something'; someone's son or daughter, someone's father or mother, someone's brother or sister, someone's aunt or uncle, someone's boss or employee, someone's something all of the time. What about me? When do I get time to be *my* me!

Listen to how people are introduced to each other and you will often hear the fact that we are somebody's something: 'This is Ann, she's John's wife.' 'This is Fred, he's Bill's father.' Yes, such introductions do have an important part to play in establishing the relationships. But what about 'me'? You must create time for that need, the need for privacy, the need to have time just for yourself. Deal with that in your life.

A secure base

One of the first principles of any accomplishment is to have a secure base. We cannot jump from sand, we can jump only from bricks. A secure base, particularly a secure relationship base, is essential for all accomplishment.

People can be great teachers, all the people we meet. We discussed role modelling, how we can find someone who would be able to do what we want to do, or someone who is already doing what we want to do, and then just do *the same*. However, everyone you meet can teach you another lesson. The skill is to listen to the information others impart and then try the ideas yourself. Some people are able to come up with great ideas but quite often don't use those ideas themselves. I have been amazed by some of the results I've had using other people's ideas. There isn't that much new in the world, just tried, tested and proven ideas presented in a different way.

Some years ago, I remember meeting a man in business and, in a fairly casual conversation, he was telling me about what was, at that time, his new banking system. He said that as he was in a cash positive business, he put all of his company's funds, every night, on the overnight money market. 'Surely one night's interest doesn't amount to that much?' I naïvely asked. 'No, it doesn't,' he replied, 'but over a year it really mounts up!'

I looked into it and he was right: it can be a small fortune if your business, and that may simply be Me Unlimited, has positive cashflow and it is usually left in a current account.

There are so many good ideas floating about, but they're just ideas if we don't investigate them for ourselves.

Never take advice on trust – even if it is offered by professionals in the field concerned. Unless you first examine it and test it, how do you know if it is good advice? So be prepared sometimes to ignore advice.

Without any criticism of bankers, accountants, solicitors or any of those professions, I always think it's a good idea to find out for yourself whether the advice they prefer is sound or not. If you are in business, you have to know how to read a set of accounts. If you use a bank, and many people do, you need to understand the banking system. Sometimes, in the commercial world, advice given by *employed* professionals may not be backed by experience at the pointed end . . . that is, by their having been in business for themselves. I heard of a bank manager of a large branch of a major bank who had retired. This was in Birmingham. He'd started his own building company and was overheard to say, 'I didn't realise all the problems that arise in business; from the safety of my office everything just looked black and white!'

Listen to advice, but check it against your own experience. Hear what has to be said, but learn as much as you can about all the systems. Who knows, maybe you know best.

Let's broaden our view for a moment. Could you describe the people you should mix with in order to be able to accomplish what you want in life? Yes, I'm sure you could. Do you mix with these people? If not, why not? Only you know the answer. However, I am sure that it is worthy of some self-management thought. If you are aiming to be a positive attitude person, then it's worth surrounding yourself with positive attitude people. It is extremely difficult to accomplish anything if those around you are 'cannot do' negative people, who are always looking at the difficulties and not the possibilities, because then we tend to become like them. Spend a holiday in a place where a different language is spoken, and within just two weeks many people are imitating the accents: it's the same principle at work. If you work abroad for any length of time, you soon pick up the mannerisms, the accents, the ways of saying things of your host country.

I have a friend, Tony, who is Italian and runs an Italian restaurant. My wife has always known when I have been speaking to him on the phone, or when I've met him. Suddenly all my words have an '-a' at the end, I'm saying 'Ciao' to people for the next hour and a half. When my father was alive, I always knew when he had watched a programme about Scotland because, although he was Scottish, he'd lived in England for most of his life and had an English accent. But whenever he watched a programme about Scotland where Scottish accents were used, his accent reverted for a while to a slight Scottish brogue.

We are all the same and if it can happen to us after just half an hour's TV, or a conversation with a friend, or just two weeks' vacation, then what happens to us if we work, play or socialise with a group? We tend to take on their accent, their positive 'can do' ways – or their negative 'cannot do' ways. If you have the decision-making power, make sure that the people in your surroundings are positive, if you want to be positive. Introduce the circuit-breaker technique, have penalties for negativity. Not only is it good fun, but the long-term impact is essential to your success.

Leadership and teamwork

These are worthy of a complete book or audio programme of their own, but, for the moment, let's examine the basics. People, I have always found, don't want to be *managed*, they want to be *led*. Nobody has ever heard of a world manager – world leader perhaps. If you are in a management role of any kind, then I suggest that you manage the tasks, but lead the people. Teach your people self-management. These are the three important attributes of leadership:

1. Leaders are 'can do' people. They are not afraid of taking action. They are pro-active, they take enthusiastic action.
2. They have confidence; confidence in themselves, confidence in their ideas, confidence in their people to be able to undertake the task in hand.
3. The 'have' vision. In Martin Luther King's unforgettable words: 'I have a dream!'

If you aim to be a leader, or you are already in a leadership role, examine your skills and abilities in these three areas: action, confidence and vision.

If you are going to be part of a team, or the leader of a team, allow a situation where people can make mistakes; it's one of the ways we all learn. Let mistakes happen without criticism of the person concerned. Some years ago I heard a story of two chief executives talking on a plane. One had turned round to the other and said that they had just had a major problem at work. One of his people had made a real foul-up; a mistake on a big computer deal.

'It cost us over a million,' said the CEO.

'What are you going to do . . . sack him?'

'Sack him! Why of course not, I've just spent over a million to train him.'

If you make mistakes in your leadership role, admit them openly and honestly; it will build the respect that the people have for you. Help your people to set and achieve their goals. A team is just like a person; if they don't know where they are going, all the roads lead there.

'TEAM – Together Everyone Achieves More.'

Have a slogan for the team, a slogan that sells the team on the team, that confirms it is a 'can do' team. Never use, in your dealings with people, that oft-used expression, 'What you have to understand is . . .' – this must be one of the worst expressions ever dreamt up, it is confrontational, it is often said in a condescending or rude manner, and people *do not* have to understand anything, they have a choice . . .

There was a study of the factors that are important to people in a working environment. The study looked at ten factors which might apply:

a Appreciation of a job well done.
b Feeling 'in' on things.
c Sympathy for personal problems.
d Job security.
e Money.
f Interesting and challenging work.
g Promotion possibilities.
h Loyalty from the company or the boss.
i Good working conditions.
j Tactful disciplining.

A large group of managers were asked to rate these factors, put them in order of importance of how they felt their people would feel. At the same time, the people in the various concerns we also asked to put the factors in order of importance; number one as the most important, through to number ten as the least important. These were the surprising results:

FACTOR	PEOPLE'S VOTE	MANAGER'S VOTE
a Appreciation	1	8
b 'In crowd'	2	10
c Sympathy	3	9
d Job security	4	2
e Money	5	1
f Interesting work	6	5
g Promotion possibilities	7	3
h Loyalty from boss	8	6
i Good conditions	9	4
j Tactful disciplining	10	7

Now, what surprised me about the study was the question of money. The managers rated it number one, but the people rated it number five. My suggestion to you, regardless of your position in your place of work, is to have that study done. I did it and was again surprised by the results. However, it enabled me to make the changes that would let people get what they wanted from the working environment, while still meeting the company's goals. Try it for yourself and see what you find out.

Improving interaction. Well, how are we going to improve our dealings, our interaction with others? First we must listen actively – *not* passively – to other people. We must use our ears and mouth in relationship to the number we have of each – two ears and one mouth – to listen for ideas, as well as the facts, that are presented by others, and to avoid jumping to conclusions but, rather, responding with a 'Yes, I see' or some such expression that lets the other person know that you are really listening. Making notes of what is said, no matter how good our memory, is a great help in active listening. We are going to cover some memory systems later.

Avoid judging people by how they say what they say. We all have different accents and sometimes it is possible to get caught up in listening to the accent rather than the content. Ask questions to make sure you understand, maintain eye contact, watch body language and what it might be saying about the person who is talking. Watch your own body language and be aware of the message you are giving out. Avoid finishing other people's sentences, and pause before you reply, to indicate that you are giving a considered response – which of course you should always be doing.

Earlier, we recognised that it is a good idea to accept that everyone is in the sales business, and understanding the basics of selling is an essential skill in our dealings with others. Open the conversation the right way, first with a positive-type response to 'How are you?' . . . 'Tremendous!'. Second, have prepared openings for important conversations. Sell the benefits of your ideas to the other person. Remember, people only ever do things for their own reasons, so we must clearly indicate the benefit to them of their acceptance of our ideas, dealing with objections that others might raise to taking the actions we are suggesting. One of the easiest ways to handle prevarication with decision-making is to use what is called The Benjamin Franklin Idea, or The Balance Sheet method. Draw a line down the centre of a piece of paper. Label the two columns 'plus' and 'minus'. List all the pros and cons, crossing off those which balance each other out. When you are left with items only under one column then the answer is obvious.

The other selling skill everyone should possess is the ability to close the sale, to ask for the order, to ask for action to be taken. Even in a commercial selling role, so many people are scared to ask for a commitment to buy and instead keep rambling on about why someone *should* buy or describing more complex features and benefits without ever actually getting to the point of saying: 'Shall we go ahead, then?' In all your selling roles, do find the right words to close. The difference between tellers and sellers is the ability to close. And this doesn't mean that you sell things to customers, or others, that they don't need or want to buy – they would soon stop being customers if you did.

Proactive. In all our dealings with other people, we need to be proactive. If we are always waiting for others to take the lead, we might have to wait a long time. Be the one to get things moving in the direction you want.

Criticism. There are times in our dealings with others when we feel that we really do have to criticise an action that has been taken, and that's the important word, the word 'action'. If we criticise the person, it's the same as praise; praising the person instead of the actions they have taken. With praise, it's just too 'gushy' to praise the person; with criticism, it's just too hard to criticise the person who took the action. Let's make sure that when the need arises, which, if we think carefully about it and the impact of our words on others, shouldn't be too often, let's make absolutely sure that it's only the action that gets the blame. It's what I call the Recognition-Repetition Principle.

Recognition-Repetition Principle. This is how it works: whatever you recognise in another person is probably what they will repeat. If you give a dog a bad name it will be a bad dog. If you give a dog a good name it will be a good dog.

When you criticise a person for the actions they have taken, the odds are that they will repeat the action. When you praise an action taken by someone, the odds are in your favour, and in their favour, that they will repeat those actions. Behavioural scientists have said that we all do things for the strokes we receive, negative strokes and positive strokes. The worst situation we can find ourselves in is receiving no strokes at all. So, if we are not praising the actions of people in our lives, and often a simple 'Thank you' is enough, then they may take action to get some negative strokes, rather than receive no strokes at all. If you are ignoring the people in your environment, whether that's work or at home, you can never be sure what actions they will take to get the strokes. Why take the risk? Give out honest praise of the actions that are taken and avoid the possibility of negative actions being taken. If you have to reprimand someone, perhaps you might try this simple five-step method.

The Five-Step Method. Make sure the reprimand takes place in private, nothing hurts more than being criticised, even if it's only for our actions, in front of our colleagues or family members.

1 Tell the person that you do like them, but don't 'gush'.
2 Let them know that you don't like 'it', 'it' not them when the actions they do take place.
3 Ask that they don't repeat the actions by explaining the consequences of the actions. Make sure that you use 'I' statements and situation statements at this stage, not accusatory-type 'you' statements.

   To explain what I mean. Say, for example, one of your children has come in late in the evening, later than arranged, and you are annoyed. Why? Maybe because you were worried. Far better to say 'I was worried about you, I rang the hospital to see if you'd been admitted', and similar 'I' type statements, than 'You don't give any thought as to how your mother and I are feeling', 'You are irresponsible', 'you', 'you', 'you'.

   So. Phrase the reprimand in the 'I', and ask them not to do it again, appeal to their better nature.
4 Mention some of the good things they do and ask them to keep doing them, but don't take too long about it. Remember: Recognition-Repetition.
5 Tell them again that you like them as a person, without getting too sentimental or over the top, and shake hands. That final touch reinforces your belief that they will, in future, live up to their and your expectations.

The Boomerang Principle. Now let's look at honesty . . . the Boomerang Principle. We know that what we sow we reap. So whatever we throw out at the world, the boomerang effect will always return to us, and often magnified, enlarged by its journey. I don't want to get heavy with this because each of us has our own game to play, our own choices for the actions we take. However, if for example someone buys something in a bar from some shady character, and they know full well it's been stolen, they can be certain that the world will pay them back.

Earl Nightingale summed it up superbly in his marvellous programme *Lead the Field*, when he said that the world is like a giant set of scales, the large brass scales which chemists used to have in their shops. The bowl on one side was labelled 'Service', the service we give to others, the way we deal with the world, the way we deal with the people in our lives; and the bowl on the other side was labelled 'Rewards', the rewards the world would give us, and the system or the force, or whatever you want to call it, would make sure that at the end of the day, the two bowls would always balance. If there's insufficient 'Stuff' in the 'Rewards' bowl, perhaps that's because the 'Service' bowl has not been filled up enough. So, let's move onto the steps:

1 Treat others as you would wish to be treated.
2 Go through the self-management exercises, looking at yourself through other people's eyes.
3 Catch yourself doing it right with the language you use with children. Remember, positive not negative.
4 Have a meeting, an open meeting, to resolve any problems. Find solutions and decide you are going to have, for example, a happy marriage, and then take action, enthusiastic action, accordingly.
5 Be aware of the people you mix with and their effect upon you.
6 Get rid of the negative people in your life, or teach them to be positive – perhaps lend them this book.
7 Use the leadership skills we discussed and get people at your place of work to do the ten-factor test.
8 Be more into active listening.
9 Start, from today, criticising only the actions, not people, using the five-step method I have outlined.
10 Remember the Boomerang Principle and have some self-management time to analyse what you are throwing out at the world.

If you take the time to go through these ideas, you'll have better, more productive, more satisfying, happier dealings with everyone in your life, if you take . . . enthusiastic action.

3 Time management

We are now going to examine one of the 'must-haves' for accomplishment – time management – though, below, I am going to refute the expression.

We are going to discuss time, a self-management test on time, 17 reasons why people run into problems with time and how to overcome those problems, the worth of our time, delegation – when to and how to – and planning; we will cover lists and how to use them to maximum effect, give five simple rules for meetings, 12 solutions and ideas to get more done each and every day; we will change our Self-talk about time, and, as always, decide on the actions and rules we are going to use; we provide ten further tips on time management, avoiding procrastination, and, finally, look at life management in terms of blocks of time.

The benefits

Well, what will be your benefits from all this information? You'll get more done, you'll be more in control of your life and time, you'll have numerous ideas to squeeze more out of each and every day and, more importantly, enjoy doing it.

Scientific tests have shown that when man is deprived of all time-measuring devices and of any natural light, he will, after a few days of disorientation, return to a functioning cycle of approximately 24 hours in length. This is called the Circadian

Rhythm (circa=about and dian=a day) – about a day. We must, therefore, have a body clock inside ourselves, and in every book, tape series, personal development lecture and seminar, there is advice on time management.

Having looked at the variety of available systems researched, the various books, tapes and seminars, experimented with paper-based and computer-based time-management programmes, I have come to a startling conclusion:

'There is no such thing as time management.'

Time is simply a perception, a convenient way in which to measure the passage of hours, days, months, seasons and years – and yet, imagine this situation:

You have an appointment with an important person for a commercial or social meeting. The appointment is, say, for 9.30 am. It will take approximately half an hour to get to the meeting, so you know you must leave your house at 9 at the latest. Being a properly planned sort of person, you set your alarm clock for 7.30, to give yourself plenty of time, an hour and a half, to get up, have breakfast, shower, get dressed etc., and leave for the meeting. During the night, your alarm clock mysteriously develops a fault and, by some miracle, advances itself by one hour. Not one hour on only the clock-face, but on the alarm setting as well. When the alarm rings and you sleepily turn over to turn it off, you notice, to your horror, that the time is apparently 8.30 am, only half an hour to get up, breakfast – although that suddenly loses its importance – shower, get dressed and leave for that important meeting. How quickly would you get out of bed? How quickly would you shower and get dressed? If it was me, very, very quickly and I'm sure you are the same. We would both be rushing around like scalded cats, and yet what has changed?

Time hasn't changed. By everyone else's clock it is still 7.30 am. What has changed is your *perception* of time.

The reverse of the situation just described also hold true: if the clock had been turned back and when it was 6.30 am we thought it was 7.30, we would still get up. Yes, we would and we would have actually gained an hour out of bed, simply through our . . . perception of time.

What conclusions, what benefits, can we have by being aware of this fact? Well, we know that the time on the clock is only a convenience of modern-day living, a universal method of measuring. We can, however, decide on our own time; in particular, our own time to get up. By so doing, *I* have found that the early hours of the morning are quieter than the rest of the day. They're an excellent time to write, prepare reports, study, plan the day, the week, the year, set goals, be creative and hundreds of other things as well. Some people say that they are morning people and have no difficulty rising, others that they are evening people and come truly alive only when the sun has slipped below the horizon. And yet, despite all that, I know that those early hours can be the most productive of times.

My suggestion to you, then, is this. Just for a few days, a few weeks, set your alarm for one hour earlier than normal, and see what happens. I know, if you are a late riser, you are saying: 'Peter, you're crazy, I need my eight hours' sleep just to function at all, lose one hour, never!' And yet, despite this, I still ask to you to try it. You will find, after a few days, that you have reduced your sleep need by one hour and that you do have one hour a day more to use as you see fit, perhaps more productively than sleeping.

While on the subject of hours, calculate what an hour a day, better used, can add up to: seven hours a week, and 365 hours a year. On the basis of ten hours a day spent doing what you do, that could mean an additional thirty-six and a half days per year. A month every year to use in a different way. You will have noticed that I didn't say 'saved', as we cannot save time, store time, put it in the bank, draw it out when we need it. We cannot revisit yesterday – physically, that is – we cannot physically live in tomorrow; we can only use each moment as it passes by.

Earlier, I said there is no such thing as time management. My main reason for saying that is that all of the solutions for the challenge of time management I've ever come across, in study and in personal use, are, in fact, not 'time-management' solutions but 'self-management' solutions, attitude solutions, self-belief solutions – but most of all, self-management solutions. I use the word solutions advisedly, because there are a great many solutions for better use of the 24 hours that everyone is allotted every day of their lives.

Let's look now at some of the problems with time and some of the solutions, and how we can accomplish more in the time available. Here is a 20-question test about the use of your time. The idea of the test is, as always, self-management. Answer the following questions with either 'often', 'sometimes' or 'seldom'. The questions score: five points for every 'often', three points for every 'sometimes' and no points for every 'seldom'. Now add up you total marks.

Self-Management Test

QUESTION	OFTEN	SOMETIMES	NEVER
1. Do you have written, up-to-date goals for your life?			
2. Do you take action on a daily basis to accomplish these goals?			
3. Do you start and finish your tasks on time?			
4. Do you allow for thinking time at work?			
5. Are you good at delegating work to others?			
6. Do people seem pleased to help you with that delegated work?			

QUESTION	OFTEN	SOMETIMES	NEVER
7. Are you punctual?			
8. Do you do your most important work at your best time of day?			
9. Can you let go of work and not be stressed or worried about it when you get home?			
10. Do you deal with interruptions effectively?			
11. Do you prepare a 'to do' list for each day?			
12. Do you put the tasks on your 'to do' list in priority order?			
13. Do you finish all the tasks on your list each day?			
14. Is your work area neat, tidy and organised?			
15. Do you put things back in their proper place?			
16. Do you handle each piece of paper only once?			
17. Do you avoid procrastination, putting things off?			

QUESTION	OFTEN	SOMETIMES	NEVER
18. Do you deal with long-winded telephone callers effectively?			
19. Is your personal filing system up to date?			
20. Are you using your time to the full?			

The purpose of this test is to focus your mind on the use of your time. If you are able to score in the area of 70 to 100 points, then you are probably doing pretty well with the use of your time. If you scored between 50 and 70, then not too bad, but maybe there are some actions you can take to improve matters. You'll know the actions to take from the answers you gave on the test.

If you are in the below 40 category, then I'm think you would agree that you are not making the best use of your most precious asset . . . time. My suggestion is that you take this test on a regular basis, taking the actions that are necessary to improve your time usage.

Perhaps some of the reason why some people have a problem with time would apply to some of the challenges you may have with time usage:

1 Negative self-image.
2 Low self-esteem.
3 Self-doubt, fear of failure, fear of making the wrong decisions.
4 Rationalisations, distractions, lack of urgency, life out of balance, no specific goals, lack of control, lack of delegation.
5 Too busy with low priority tasks.
6 Procrastination (putting things off 'til tomorrow).
7 Poor self-management skills.

Well, how can we overcome these problems? First, I think we need to accept that hard work is not always the answer. Many people rush around, apparently busy, but accomplishing nothing at all. The answer is *smart* work, doing only the things that bring the results that you want. Dealing with interruptions is a prime example.

Dealing with interruptions. The first thing to do is to analyse the types of interruption that stop you performing. Are they telephone interruptions or physical interruptions? If they are telephone interruptions, then make sure you have a screening process; this could be a secretary, a switchboard operator or even an answering machine on your desk or voice-mail, so that you speak only to the callers you want to speak to *when* you want to speak to them.

Let people know when you do not want to be disturbed. A system I've used for an office environment is to issue each person with a sign that simply says, 'I'm busy, please do not interrupt me unless it's urgent.' This was placed at a strategic place on the desk, chair or office door.

Some years ago, I remember seeing, in a magazine, a small picture of a tramp watching a Rolls Royce go by. In the Rolls Royce was a man sitting in the back, relaxing – it was a chauffeur-driven car – and the tramp was saying: 'Ah, there but for *me* go I.'

It's true, isn't it – time management is really self-management. 'There but for *me* go I.'

People use the word 'spend' about time, as though they were spending money. In effect we are. 'Time is money' is a well-used phrase. It is how we spend it that is important. Time cannot be put on the shelf and used tomorrow, we cannot shorten or lengthen time, we cannot borrow it or lend it, we cannot even work harder and earn some more of it. We have to self-manage.

If we are able, by good self-management, to increase our available time for accomplishing the things we wish to accomplish by saving for better use just 10% of the time we use, then the amount available to us for that accomplishment over a period of years is staggering. Just think: six minutes per hour over a ten-hour day would be 60 minutes, one whole hour. One hour per day for 365 days, another month to put to better use. With life expectancy in the 70 years bracket, that could be six years extra. Add to that getting up one hour earlier every day, and it could be *12* extra years . . .

Let's now look at the cost of your time, so that you can clearly focus on the monetary gain, or loss, of good self-management of your time. For every £10 000 you earn, per annum, including or excluding car and expenses, bonuses, and based on a normal ten-hour working, or playing, day, at 300 days per annum, you receive £3.33 per hour. So, if you are on £50 000 per year, that's £16.65 per hour, and that's only the pay you receive – it's not usually the worth of your time.

If your time is used at a place of work, the charge-out cost of that time might be three, five or ten times the basic figure. For our example, let's use five times, at £50 000 per annum: that's a charge-out time of around £80 per hour.

Where does this lead us? Well, the first thing it must lead us to is to examine the tasks we do to see if they are worth this amount. The famous Pareto rule says that 80% of our results comes from 20% of our efforts, that 80% of sales come from 20% of the sales force, that 80% of our income, as businesses, comes from 20% of the clients. We must therefore examine the tasks with this in mind. Are the tasks worth the cost of your time and, if they are not, delegate them; use the Four Ds Principle: Do it, Delegate it, Dump it or Diary it. Because if you can't, won't or can't afford to do it, and you cannot delegate it to someone who will or can afford, because of their pay structure, to do it, then you might as well dump it, because it isn't going to get done.

The fourth D stands for Diary it, and this is for the small number of tasks that you want to do at some time in the future, now is not their time. Have a section in your day-planner or diary called 'Don't forget' in which to put these tasks, in brief note form, and review the section from time to time to see if the tasks have moved up in priority. Other than that, you could diary appropriate paperwork in a 1 to 31 file, which we cover later.

Delegation

Delegation can be a difficult thing. Many people like to think that there are certain things that only they can do. I'm sure that's right! There are certain things that only you can do, but are they all the things you do? I think we should delegate more often.

Delegate the task if someone can do it less expensively and just as well; delegate the task if someone likes to do it more than you like doing it – they'll probably do it better! And delegate if someone can do it faster than you.

Direction for delegation

1. Downwards; people in our teams, or people we lead. When delegating downwards, we must remember to delegate the authority to get the task done as well. It's often good to delegate the result rather than the process. Let people know what you want as an outcome, rather than *how* to do the job; presumably you have delegated the task because they can do it, so . . . let them do it and simply delegate the result you require.
2. Sideways: to people holding similar positions to yourself, other team members, other managers and other directors.
3. Upwards: if you are a member of a team and you have a boss of some description, perhaps you could delegate some tasks upwards to the person with the authority to get the job done.

With all delegation, make sure that a time-frame for the completion of the task has been set. With your people, this may be a well-phrased command. With your peers or the boss, this would take the form of a question, such as: 'When will you be able to get back to me with the results (or answer)?'

Most people these days have a diary or day-planner of some description and that can be a great help in self-management in relation to time. I use a four-ring binder which I have prepared for myself, called 'Time Tracker', which has space for do-lists and telephone calls and overview sections for the week and month, together with life-management sections and a long-term do-list. It works well. If you don't have such a system, it might be worth looking at them, or designing one of your own.

The way we can solve our problems with time is to go back to the basics. First, you need to know how you currently *spend* your time. This sounds simple, but it is not always easy . . . it means the preparation of a timelog. If you've never done a timelog before, it is slightly more difficult than it first appears, and that isn't being negative, it's being realistic.

So, using the pages which follow, copy these, or photocopy them, and then decide on the day you will do your timelog. During that day, record, in the spaces provided, what you were doing in each of the half-hour segments of the day. This note needs to be brief but clear. At the start of the next day, analyse what – I suggest you use a code system that is simple, perhaps using only four codes: A, B, C and D. Any more than that at this stage and you may find it too difficult to analyse the results. You could use code A for your prime activity, code B for a slightly less important activity – maybe travelling time not used in any other way – code C for the things you think you might have been able to delegate or to social time, and code D is for time you believe you wasted.

Timelog

Name: ______________________________

Date: ______________________________

07:00 ______________________________

07:30 ______________________________

08:00 ______________________________

08:30 ______________________________

09:00 ______________________________

09:30 ______________________________

10:00 ______________________________

10:30 ______________________________

11:00 ______________________________

11:30 ______________________________

12:00 ______________________________

12:30 ______________________________

13:00 ____________________
13:30 ____________________
14:00 ____________________
14:30 ____________________
15:00 ____________________
15:30 ____________________
16:00 ____________________
16:30 ____________________
17:00 ____________________
17:30 ____________________
18:00 ____________________
18:30 ____________________
19:00 ____________________
19:30 ____________________
20:00 ____________________
20:30 ____________________
21:00 ____________________
21:30 ____________________
22:00 ____________________
22:30 ____________________
23:00 ____________________
23:30 ____________________
24:00 ____________________

This simple idea will really let you know how you spend your time. There should be sufficient information from a typical day for you to be able to draw some conclusions and take the appropriate actions.

If there isn't, you might change your segments to one hour and do a timelog for a number of days. You will be able to incorporate the cost of your time, as we have previously calculated, by examining the tasks or activities for your day and the amount of time you spend on them and therefore the cost of those tasks. For example, you may have decided that you charge your time out at, say, £80 per hour. However, you spent two hour during the day doing tasks that were worth only £40 per hour – that may be poor use of your time. If you have people in your teams, or people under your control in the working environment, I would suggest that you have a timelog done at least one day every month to enable the team members to see where their time is being spent and make better decisions regarding the use of their time. This is particularly important with a sales team, in order to find out how much of each day is actually spent selling.

As we are discussing teams and time, the other area I believe we should look at is: what effect do you have on the time of your team? What effect do they have on your time? If there are problems in these areas, how can you change, or how can you persuade the team members to change? Remember, you are probably involved in a number of teams, at home and at work.

Sometimes, some people can think that planning their time can make them too rigid. I have found that the opposite is the case; planning gives flexibility. Just because you plan things out doesn't mean that the plan is carved in stone – it's your plan, you can change it as you see fit. However, having a plan in the first place gives you direction and makes you more aware of yourself and your surroundings, and what you really want to accomplish in a given period of time.

'It wasn't raining when Noah built the Ark.'

Plan each week during the preceding weekend, have a plan for all the areas of your life; we'll move on to life management in a moment. Use the do-list idea. This idea was created earlier this century by a management consultant by the name of Ivy Lee, who'd been asked to help the CEO of a major company. He suggested to the CEO that he write down on a piece of paper the six most important things that had to be done the following day, to put those items in order and put the list back in his pocket. Lee then suggested that, when the CEO arrive at work the following day, he take the list out of his pocket and start work on item number one on the list, running through the items on the list until all completed as far as he was concerned. The CEO could then reprioritise the list and move on to the new item number one. Ivy Lee told the CEO to use the idea for a number of weeks and then send him a cheque for whatever he thought it was worth. A few months later, he received a cheque for $25 000 (this was in 1930!) – imagine how much that would be worth today. Someone paid highly for this idea and it is here for anyone to use.

I have used do-lists for many years and can confirm to you that if you are not a do-list user, it is one of the simplest and most effective time-usage tools I have ever come across. The important part is not only to write out the list, but to put the items in order; that's what makes the difference. If you don't currently use do-lists, I urge you to try them and prove that the CEO's money – and your time – was well spent.

Meetings

These are obviously a time-consuming area for so many businesses and people. Here are five ideas to improve all of your meetings:

1. Calculate, before the meeting takes place, the cost of the meeting. First, the in-cost – that is to say, the actual salary cost of those attending for the hours the meeting will take – and then the charge-out cost of the time of those people. If the meeting is going to have to bear a cost of, say, £500, will the meeting be worthwhile, or could it have fewer attendees, or take less time?
2. Always prepare an agenda for the meetings and have the agendas circulated before the meetings. This allows people to say 'You don't need me for this meeting' or 'You only need me for item three on the agenda, what time will item three be discussed?' It also allows people to prepare for the meeting and that can save an inordinate amount of time at the meeting itself.
3. Think carefully about the time of day at which you are going to have the meeting. I have often found that meetings that begin at 5.30 pm are over a lot quicker than the same meeting beginning at 10.00 am.

4. Have firm chairing of the meeting, firm not harsh. Firm chairing will ensure that everyone there has their say without constant repetition of the ideas. Ask questions to each individual such as, 'Have you anything to add?' – emphasing the 'add'. By asking direct questions, you involve those who are reluctant to speak but who might may have some good ideas. The person who is to chair the meeting and the agenda should clearly state the deadline for the ending of the meeting; this will keep people on track.
5. Have an action list that is prepared for the meeting so that everyone leaves knowing what they must accomplish before the next meeting, setting deadlines for the actions. There is nothing like peer pressure to get actions completed from meetings.

Other solutions for time usage include studying the procedures undertaken by you and others, and seeing if there is a better way to do the job. It could be that you, or they, have always done the job a particular way, but that time has changed the situation and a new procedure would be more time-effective.

Look at people's job descriptions: do they clearly indicate the results as well as the functions that are required? Could it be that someone is carrying out their job function, but not meeting the results you expect, simply because they do not know what the results are supposed to be, they know only the functions?

Allocate chunks of time during the working day for a special appointment, the appointment with the 'president' of Me Unlimited. Make sure that this time is so special that it would take a real emergency to have you cancel the appointment. Use these chunks for thinking time, planning time and goals-setting time. Often, thinking is the most productive thing we do and we're frequently paid more for our thoughts than our actions – especially if in a leadership or directorship role.

Saying 'No'

I've previously mentioned some people's inability to say 'No' and it may possibly be a self-esteem problem. If you've found yourself, in the past, saying 'Yes' where you wished you'd said 'No', try an idea I used some years ago, when it worked extremely well. Go to you day-planner or diary and write the word 'No' on every evening for the rest of the year. Now this is not to say that when you're asked if you can make an event, social or commercial, for that evening, you will always say 'No'; it just reminds you that you *can* say 'No', 'No, thank you'. I was surprised how many thing I did go to, even though I had the word 'No' in my diary, but also surprised at how many things I didn't go to and didn't miss. If the end of the year is a long way away, try it for just one month and see what happens.

Eight ideas for better time usage

1 Keep a 1–31 file. This is simply 31 hanging files kept in a filing cabinet. The files are labelled 1 to 31, representing the 31 days of the month. When you have to diary forward a piece of correspondence in order to phone someone back on a particular day, put it in the appropriate file. When you want a particular piece of paper on a particular day, put it in the file and then just check the files every day. Check that day's file at the start of every day or at the end of the previous day. Sometimes this has been called a 'tickler' file, because it 'tickles' your memory. If you do not need a piece of paperwork for, say, three months, still put it in the numbered file corresponding with the day and just ignore it until the appropriate month comes around. If you have long-term correspondence that may not need to be checked for a year, do exactly the same.

2 An ideas file. This can be kept in your filing cabinet or at the back of your diary or day-planner. We all have flashes of inspiration from time to time and this is a great way to keep

the ideas for the moment when their time has come. I find that as I add new ideas to my ideas file, the reading of some of the old ideas links in to some of the new ideas and even more ideas come to mind.

3 People files. If you have people to whom you speak on a regular basis or with whom you tend to have regular meetings, keep a file for them and as each day proceeds and items come up that need to be discussed with these people, keep notes in the file. This avoids having lots of telephone conversations or meetings, each worth its own pleasantries or greetings, 'Good mornings' or 'Goodbyes'. Have one telephone call, one meeting.

4 A tidy desk. There is an old joke that says that a tidy desk is the sign of a sick mind – and it is just that . . . an old joke. If we are working on a particular project and our desk or work areas are cluttered with other papers or products with which we have to deal, our eyes wander and as they do our minds wander. It is essential, if you have a great deal of paperwork around, to have two desks, or two work areas, one with the papers, preferably behind you, and one with the current project paperwork, in front of you. That way you can remain extremely focused on the job in hand.

5 Magazines. One of the massive time-users is the number of business, trade or industry magazines we receive, and feel that we should read. Here's a thought: instead of stacking them up for a final clearout one Saturday morning, just look through the contents in the front of the magazine and tick the items that interest. Scan those items and tear out the pages, file them in the appropriate file and throw the magazine away.

The other thing that you really should read, in all magazines, is the adverts, because there is something to be learned from each one. If you read each advert and understand why you might possibly respond to that advert, then you may be able to use that information in your own business. This is why it is a good idea to read all direct mail, in order to find out what parts of that direct mail create response, so that they can be utilised in your business.

6 Letters. This idea can not only save you time but also save your secretary a lot of time. There are many letters we receive where we can reply on the letter itself; for example, with letters that ask us a question or a series of questions, simply write your reply on the front or back of the letter; where it says (at the top of the page) your name, write in large letters 'FROM:', and where it says the name of the person who sent you the letter (at the bottom of the page), write in large letters 'TO:'. Take a photocopy of the letter after you have made your comments and return the original to the sender. This may seem to be against normal ideas. However, I've never had anyone object and the time made available for other activities can be quite substantial.

7 Dictating machine. It would be wise for everyone to invest in a dictating machine. First, for dictating letters, and secondly, for capturing ideas as they come to mind.

8 The Napoleon Principle. If you have people in your work team who come to you for solutions to problems, then a good idea is to install the process known as The Napoleon Principle. It was said that when Napoleon's people came to him with a problem, they would have to come with three solutions. Make that the rule for your people. If they are the ones directly involved with the problem, chances are that they probably know the solutions as well. They may be looking only for your approval of the solutions they have already worked out. Ask them to bring three solutions with every problem and ask them which one they think is the action to take.

If you have someone to whom you report, perhaps the next time you go with a problem, you could also go with solutions. She or he may pleasantly surprised at your forethought.

Ten further tips on time

1 As Mark Twain once said:

'If you have to eat a frog, don't look at it too long.'

We know what he meant by this; just get on and do it. Simply looking at the problem or that piece of paper won't make it go away, so use the Four Ds Principle.

2 Tidy your desk or work area last thing before leaving work in the evening.
3 Do your thinking on paper. Using paper for thinking isn't a waste of time, it's an effective use of time.
4 If you're an early morning person, perhaps you could arrange the day so that you can go into work early and leave early. If you're an evening type, perhaps you might go in later and leave later. This could result in your being able to do your most important work at your best time.
5 Regardless of preferred time, everyone has energy drops, like just before lunch when the body needs food and just after lunch when the body is using available energy to digest food. To avoid the after-lunch feeling, whenever possible eat a light lunch.
6 If you have clients, customers or people to whom you write regularly, set up a system with them that brief, to-the-point letters are acceptable. For example, it has always been my habit after meetings with clients to write and confirm the details discussed, thanking them for their time and scheduling actions that we have agreed to take. One of my clients was Managing Director of a bank-affiliated leasing company and we would have regular lunches and meetings. The letters seemed to take on the same tones and were often more courtesy that content. One day I wrote to him:

Dear Stuart,
Usual letter.
Sincerely,
Peter

He though it was great and it became our system.

7 The same idea could work for telephone calls. With very regular callers, perhaps you could have an arrangement for no social chit-chat – just down to business and one goodbye. Listen to people around you; you can hear some of them

saying goodbye on the phone up to ten times. Just think of the time that's wasted.

8 If you have to spend a great deal of time at one place of work, for example sitting at your desk or work station, try to make the work fit into two or three different height levels. You might have a drawing board at which you stand and a desk at which you sit. Different levels give a different perspective and relieve strain from sitting or standing in one place for too long.

9 If you are going to have a meeting that will take travelling time, phone before you go. In these days when nigh on everyone has a mobile phone of some description, it's a great idea to phone on the way to check that some emergency or change of plans hasn't taken the person you were going to see away from the meeting place.

Nothing is worse than travelling for two hours to see someone who is out. Not only does it lose you two hours there, it loses you two hours back, possibly in an angry or disappointed mood.

10 If you are working on a project and you have come to a difficult part, rather than getting stuck on that bit, jump over it, leave it altogether and return to it later. By this I do not mean procrastinate; if it must be done, we need to do it. I mean in a situation where something just doesn't seem to be working, maybe by moving forward in the project the solution will suddenly become clear, it will suddenly fit into place.

Before we move on to our life-management quiz and the matter of avoiding procrastination, let's just examine the self-talk that goes on about time.

We must not be the victims of others, or ourselves, if we are going to use our time effectively. You will, I'm sure, have heard people say the following, and I've translated from the victim-style language into what's really happening:

'I don't have time to achieve my goals.'
= 'I don't make time available to use my goals.'

'I'm always being interrupted.'
= 'I allow people to interrupt me.'

'There is never time to do the things I want to do.'
= 'I'm letting other people decide my rules and actions.'

'He always keeps me on the phone for ages.'
= 'I let him keep me on the phone for ages.'

As always, we get a choice. It is our time, it is your time.

Procrastination

> *'Procrastination is the thief of time.'*

This is a common expression and I am sure that it is right. Why do people procrastinate? Why do people put off things they know they should do, or know they want to do, until a different time or different day?

Fear. Fear of failure, fear of success, fear of embarrassment. They hope that, if they procrastinate, the task will go away. They are living their lives by other people's rules and they have not associated enough gain or pain to the situation. What are the results of procrastination?

Frustration, your reputation suffers, your self-esteem goes down, your confidence goes down. We become known as a 'Cannot do' person or a 'Will not do' person in the eyes of others and in our own eyes as well; there is an attitude change from positive to negative . . . we create a vicious circle . . . I don't do things therefore I am a negative person, I'm a negative person therefore I don't do things.

Well, here's a very simple system to beat procrastination – it's called The Salami Principle. I've heard it on so many tapes and read about it in so many books on time and negotiation, I've heard it discussed at so many meetings and seminars, and though I don't know where it originated, it's a great idea.

Imagine you have gone to a delicatessen, and there hanging in the window is a large salami. Well, you may like salami, but can you imagine a situation where you would be able to eat the whole thing in one go . . . It would be far easier if you asked the shopkeeper to take the salami and put it on his slicing machine and slice it into thin slices; that way – particularly if you like salami – you'd still be able to eat the whole thing, but one slice at a time. That's the Salami Principle and this is how we use it:

1 Make a decision.
First then, make a decision that you *will do* whatever it is that you have been putting off. Use the power of questions, the Subconscious Encoding Process of self-management. Ask the following question on paper . . . it must be on paper:
'What do I need to . . .?'
Remember, your mind now accepts that you are going to do it, that the decision has been made. Then, write down the list of actions that you know must be taken to get the job completed. These are the pieces of the salami.

2 Prioritise.
Prioritise the list by putting in order the actions that you must take.

3 The Carpet Fitter's Technique.
This part I have added to the Salami Principle. Years ago, I was talking to a carpet fitter – he was fitting some carpets in my house. He had been a carpet fitter for many, many years. It was a pleasure to watch him work. I said to him: 'Do you ever cut the carpet in the wrong place?'
'Never,' was his response.
'Never?' I replied.
He responded: 'We always measure it twice and cut it once, that way we never have to cut it twice if we measure only once.'
I realised what an excellent process this was and have used it ever since when it comes to prioritising actions. You can use it in the same way.

Having prioritised your list of actions, now all you need to do is to prioritise it again. This is my suggestion: do the first prioritisation on the right-hand edge of the paper, then fold that edge under so you cannot see it. Then . . . prioritise again. After that, unfold the paper and check the two lists. If they are in the same order, great! If not, maybe you can use the ideas that will have sprung to mind by measuring the list twice. Here's a tip: if the list is so long that it's extremely difficult to put it in any sort of reasonable order, start by deciding if an action is rated as 'A', 'B' or 'C'. 'A' are the group of first actions, 'B' the group of second actions, and 'C' obviously the group of last actions. Then put each group into order; now you know the actions you have to take. This is the time to confirm to yourself that you are going to do the task. It could be that having decided on the actions, you decide that the result is not worth your cost, or that the job doesn't need doing at all, or that it needs delegating. If, however, you have decided to do it, take the first action now if at all possible. That gets the whole thing moving, and that one step also creates direction.

Decide on a reward. You will recall that, as human beings, we take action to avoid pain and gain pleasure, so now is the time to decide on the reward you will have, the pleasure you will have, by completing the list of actions. If it was redecorating a room in your house, perhaps you could arrange a party: that's commitment and reward. If it's a task that will make you money, decide how you will spend the money.

Handling Paper

One of the simplest ways to avoid handling a piece of paper many times is to use the Measles Principle. The Measles Principle is easy to use; every time you handle a piece of paper, put a red dot on it; keep putting dots on it every time you handle it, and you will soon realise how many times you handle those bits of paper that really should be dealt with straight away.

Life management

You can undertake this exercise using the pages provided. It will take about 15 minutes to half an hour to complete and it will, in my opinion, be some of the best time you have ever spent.

I'd like you to think of your life as though it were divided into seven sections, seven blocks. It's been said that our minds like to deal with blocks of information and that seven blocks is about the maximum number with which we can effectively cope. Here are some areas you could consider:

Love and Affection, Self-Development, Old Skills, New Skills, Health, Exercise, Diet, Financial Management, Learning, Legal and Financial Matters, House, Holidays, Family, Friendships, Projects, Sports, Career, Travel, Relationships, Writing, Social Activities, Partners, Pets, Reading, Children, Television, Shopping . . . I'm sure there's many more.

So, divide your life into seven main areas; there is no need to put them in priority order. Next, in the first percentage column, decide on the amount of time you would *wish* to spend in each of these areas and put it in percentage terms; 5% for this area, 60% for that area – whatever percentage of your time you would *wish* to spend in those seven areas.

Life Management Test

Life Areas	%	%
1.		
2.		
3.		
4.		
5.		
6.		
7.		

Example Areas

Old Skills	Legal	Friendships	Writing
New Skills	Learning	Projects	Partner
Health	Pets	Sports	Reading
Exercise	House	Love & Affection	TV
Diet	Holidays	Self-Development	Work
Financial	Shopping	Management	etc.
Children	Work	Career	

Now that you have done that, I want you to give thought to and then calculate – the amount of time you *actually* spend in each of those areas. The question is: are those percentages the same? Are you actually spending your time as you want or wish to spend it? If not, why not?

By using the focusing test during my various in-house and open seminars, I have found that many people do not have their desires balanced with what is actually happening in their life. It is often that the work time is high on the actual 'Spent Time' column, but lower on the 'Desired Time' column. It is often that home or family or children is high on the 'Desired Time' column but low on the 'Spent Time' column. What can you do? Well, you are the boss of Me Unlimited, you have a choice.

There are now decisions to be made. One way to resolve any imbalance is to change what you do; another way is to change what you wish; however, you have to make the decision. Take control of your life and times.

I am thankful to TMI, the Time Management company, for giving me their permission to share the following poem by Alice Chase with you. I think it has relevance to how we spend our time. It is called 'To My Grown Up Son':

My hands were busy through the day,
I didn't have much time to play;
The little games you asked me to,
I didn't have much time for you.

I'd wash your clothes, I'd sew and cook,
But when you'd bring me your picture book,
And ask me please to share your fun,
I'd say a little later son.

I'd tuck you in all safe at night,
And hear your prayers, turn out the light,
Then tiptoe softly to the door,
I wish I'd stayed a minute more.

For life is short and years rush past,
A little boy grows up so fast;
No longer is he is at your side,
His precious secrets to confide.

The picture books are put away,
There are no children's games to play,
No goodnight kiss, no prayers to hear,
That all belongs to yesteryear.

My hands once busy now lie still,
The days are long and hard to fill;
I wish I might go back and do,
The little things you asked me to.

The steps for self-management of time

1. Take the Self-management 20-questions test on a regular basis, adding other questions which you feel will help you realise how you are using your time.
2. Go through the list of 17 reasons why people have problems with time, realise which ones have been giving you problems, and decide what you are going to do.
3. Set up your system to handle interruptions.
4. Calculate the cost of your time per hour.
5. Do a timelog on a regular basis.
6. Do a list of tasks you perform regularly with a value for each,

and decide which tasks in future you will delegate or dump.

7 Spend some time to look at the teams in your life and the effects on your time and your effect on their time.
8 Use the five ideas on meetings to have better, more productive, less expensive meetings.
9 Go though the list of suggested solutions and tips again and make notes of those which are relevant to you, to enable you to get more things done.
10 Obtain or design a good diary or day-planner with weekly, monthly and yearly overviews.
11 Decide now to use a do-list every single day, and that you will prioritise the items on it.
12 If watching TV is a problem, make a commitment for just one week to watch only programmes you have recorded (other than the news).
13 Change your self-talk about your In-talk about time; avoid being a victim.
14 Use the Salami Principle, allied to the Carpet Fitter's technique, to avoid procrastination.
15 Use the Life-management time allocation method on a regular basis, to ensure that you are spending time in the areas in which you wish to spend your time and that you are living by your rules and not someone else's.

All of these steps are going to take *time*, but the benefits are enormous, and with self-management of your time you are guaranteed to accomplish more and more and more, as always by taking . . . enthusiastic action.

4 Goal-setting

The world is into goal-setting, isn't it? Well, if the people I meet are anything to go by, the world isn't into goal-setting, yet 'everybody' says it is essential. It is.

'If you don't know where you're going, all the roads lead there.'

The usual goal-setting exercise takes so long to prepare and undertake that many people give up before they complete it and prove to themselves that goal-setting isn't for them. I've set so many goals which I *haven't* accomplished, that I've lost count of them; diet goals, weight goals nearly reached until dinner with a major client blew them away. Saving goals had to be spent to satisfy some unplanned bill. Yet despite all of these results (some would call them failures), goal-setting does work. For I've also lost count of the goals I *have* achieved through setting them.

To set goals, we need to go slowly, take everything one step at a time – unless that small inner voice tells us to go all out for something; then just do it. We know that there are no failures in life, just results, results from which we learn. Every attempt is a lesson learnt, writing it down makes it come true. Our attitude is that if goals are to be accomplished, then they will be. If not, their time, your time, hasn't yet come, provided you gave it your all.

During this section on goal-setting, we are going to cover a number of things. First, what I call 'Crossing the Chasm', six methods to get you from where you are now to where you want to be. Next, a little mental arithmetic problem to focus on goal-setting, a look at reasons why people don't set goals or don't update their goals as often as they might. This will help you establish your reasons for setting goals. Then there's the Lottery Principle and how it relates to goal-setting and, more importantly, goal-achieving. Twelve areas in which you might wish to set goals are indicated, with a simple plan to set the goals that you want so that you can create a direction in your life, so that you can be in control. Why it's important to establish the purpose of your goals is defined, while the Yesterday's Road philosophy will help you decide upon the actions you need to take in order to accomplish your goals.

We discuss affirmations, subliminals and the reticular activation system, and how all of these will ensure that you do hit the targets you set for yourself. We look at the obstacles that can get in the way and how planning for them can diminish the likelihood of your being knocked off track. We examine two record-keeping systems and how they can keep you on track. Naturally, we also cover self-talk, In-talk programming and the 12 steps to becoming a goal-setter and goal-achiever. Finally, not that you need it by now, a little bit more pressure to take . . . enthusiastic action.

The first step across the chasm

The problem some people experience in the setting of goals or targets is that of making a decision. They know where they are now, but they don't know where they want to be, not in detail. I think that many other people do have an idea, though, however vague. They might want success, but not have a definition. And money, but they've never decided how much. Happiness, too – but what is it that makes them happy? And then peace of mind – but how are the words to be interpreted?

Why do people have these problems? I think the following will help. Imagine a decision needs to be made, whatever the situation. That decision will involve you in action, action that takes you from where you are now to where you want to be. In between here and there, or if you will . . . now and then, there is a void, a chasm, a deep black hole. It's daunting to take the first step, in case you fall into the chasm, or there is no way back to the position that you're in now.

For example, a sales manager just cannot understand why his salespeople, who possess all the skills to sell more, increase their results, increase their earnings, be well-regarded, have success in the eyes of their peer-group, etc., etc., just don't use their skills. The answer lies in the Crossing the Chasm Principle. The salesperson is rightly scared that if he or she decides to attempt to jump from where they are now, across that unknown space, to success and more sales, and fails – even by a small amount – then they will fall into the chasm, there will be no way back to today's position. What's the answer?

Well, there are a number of answers and solutions, some or all of which will work for you:

1 The first rule is easy to say, but harder to do than all the others – be scared, but do it anyway. I remember going once to a woodlands adventure playground with my children. It was an outdoor activity centre with log-built slides, rope bridges and climbing areas all made of logs and wood – a great place for children, and, even better, the adults were allowed to go on almost everything as well.

One of the activities was called 'The Death Slide!' – now there's a reverse sell if ever I saw one, The Death Slide. Anyway, it was a steel cable stretched between two trees in a wood, about 50 yards between the trees. Over the cable was a small metal pulley-wheel and hanging from the wheel was a chain with a round rubber flat platform to sit on. The idea was simple enough; climb up on this log about four feet in the air, reach up, grab the chain, keep your fingers out of the pulley-wheel, leap upwards and forwards and, with luck, wrap your legs around the lower part of the chain and sit on the 12-inch diameter flat piece of rubber, easy – Huh! – of course. Then the pulley would slide down the cable at an ever-increasing rate of knots with you dangling underneath, gripping on for grim death – obviously the reason for the name, The Death Slide. Hurtling down 50 yards of cable until you suddenly came to a stop by the pulley-wheel hitting a buffer, which in turn would throw you forwards, feet first, until your back was facing the ground and then you would slowly come to a halt and jump off, with ground about three feet below you, making sure that your chin didn't get 'clonked' by the rubber seat on the way down.

Easy? Or perhaps not?

However, rule number one came into play: be scared and do it anyway. I climbed on to the log platform, jumped and whizzed off down the slide. Scared? No, it was great!! I felt like Indiana Jones in *The Last Crusade*, when he had to step out into the void and just believe that there would be a way across the chasm. Once you were on it, it was so much fun, so much slower than it appeared from the safety of firm ground. The banging into the buffer was nothing, it was super, it was so good. I had to go again again and again – and that's from a man who doesn't go on circus rides – blind panic, fun to be paid for! The moral? Sometimes there isn't a choice, you just have to go for things and hope they turn out OK. With most things in life, they do. Just think how many things we might have tried; businesses we could have started, relationships we might have enjoyed, food that might have tasted great – and so much more – all missed because we simply didn't try.

2 Build a bridge

Build a bridge of steps across the gap – the gap from where you are now to where you want to be. Success always comes one step at a time, so what 'one step' could you take towards that destination?

- The first step is to decide on the destination.
- Then decide you are going to make the journey.
- Next decide on, or realise, the rewards of reaching the other side.

- If you are faltering, remind yourself of other chasms you have crossed safely and successfully. Rope bridges with planks do sway – hold on tight.
- Decide what other steps need to be taken, but one step at a time. If you are halfway across and decide you don't like what you see on the other side, come back. You will and have learned something. Decide perhaps on another direction and go through the same process. In the meantime, you – your mind, your brain, your body – will have learned valuable lessons that could be applied to crossing loads of chasms. But a word of warning: don't give up too easily, look at the benefits of crossing to the other side, hang on, don't take too many steps at a time unless circumstances clearly indicate that you should – just one step at a time towards your interpretation of success.

3 Have a safety net or a safety rope tied around your waist

If you are in management or leadership of people of any kind then I believe you need this method. It works wonderfully for ourselves and wonderfully for our people. We need to know that if we try to cross that gap and fall – note I didn't say 'fail' – that there will be a way back to the start, a safety net to fall on or a safety rope to haul us back without major injury. For leaders, the net or rope is the knowledge by their people that trying and falling doesn't get them fired, that trying and falling isn't the end of their job, their income, their security. As a leader you have to tell them that the net is in place. It doesn't go against my idea of 'Burning the Bridges', it's just another method which can be used so that we have a complete set of ideas, methods and techniques for all situations. None are right, none are wrong; all are right, all are wrong – depending on the circumstances. If one method doesn't get you across, try another until you find the one that works for you and works for your people. That net or rope for ourselves when we're self-managing or self-leading is the simple realisation that in certain circumstances there is very little to lose by trying, that there are occasions in life where it is better to have tried, just for the experience, rather than not try. If things don't work out we have lost nothing of value, but we have gained the invaluable asset of experience.

4 Holding hands

Take someone with you, someone who has crossed the chasm before. It's that old expression:

'If you want to know the way up the mountain, ask someone who has travelled the road.'

As a manager or leader, go across the chasms with your people, either across the bridge one step at a time, or in one big jump holding hands.

Remember *Butch Cassidy and the Sundance Kid*, when they were at the top of the mountain and the posse was climbing towards them; only one way to go: jump hundreds of feet into the river below. 'After you,' said Sundance. 'No, after you,' said Cassidy. Together, holding hands, they leap to safety and freedom to fight another day. Hold hands, albeit mentally, with someone who has already travelled, or someone who is going your way. In a team, let's all go together, the company won't sack us all, will they? As a leader, show your team by example that the journey can be made and that you are going to support them, going to guide them and help them along the way, after all . . .

'A good example is worth a hundred times good advice.'

I remember at my wedding to my wife Sharon, my best man was so nervous, so jumpy that I had to be strong, I had to be the confident one. I asked him afterwards if he had done it on purpose, was it his technique. 'No,' he replied. 'Pete, I was shaking in my boots.'

Is there someone shaking in their boots who also wants to go where you're going? Could you help them and by so doing, make the crossing yourself?

5 The rules

This embraces all the others and we have covered it in various parts of this book. Decide on the rules. Remember, we all work for Me Unlimited, we set the rules, so set your rules for the crossing. Bring up the floor of the chasm until it's only one foot from the top and any fall is only a stumble. Decide that you cannot fail, even if you stumble, that to fail would take so many things to happen in a such an unusual sequence that it just isn't possible. For example, the gap you want to cross is from where you are now (no loving relationships) to the other side (a long-term relationship with a wonderful person).

One rule for failure could be: I need to have asked out for dinner – and been rejected – by ten thousand people. When I ask, it's only failure if the person I ask throws a five gallon bucket of purple paint over my head could be another. When I approach someone, they turn into Medusa, with snakes for hair and one look from their eyes turns me to stone, or . . . any other rules . . . you decide, it's your life, you have the right to set your own rules.

6 A role model

As we have discussed more than once already, have a role model, someone who has already done what you want to do, somebody who has achieved the goals that are the same as yours. Find someone who has done it and either do it the way they did it – that way you know you cannot fall, because they didn't fall – or go and ask them how to do it – successful people are invariably only too pleased to help in this way. I have done this; I won't go into details of the people, that wouldn't be right, but I am indebted to so many successful people who, on a simple request, were prepared to share a lifetime of chasm-crossing experiences with me and, in many cases, helped me across.

So how are we going to get you from where you are now to where you want to be? First, you need to know where you want to be, that's going to be the goal-setting part of this session. If you are in leadership, use the methods for yourself and with your people. Let's widen our view of goal-setting to include some of the goals we could set – and actually how to set them. Success isn't in short supply, there is plenty of it out there in the world, all we have to do is and decide which bit of it we want and go out and get it. Goals can be anything we decide: big goals, small goals, goals to learn new skills, to visit far-off lands, to have a happy marriage, to be or do or have anything our hearts or minds desire – you have the choice.

Think back, for a moment, to say five years ago; how old were you then? What goals did you have in you life for the next five years, the period up to today? Have you accomplished them yet? Have you realised your dream? No? Well, is it likely then that in five years more, without a plan, without goal-setting of some description, you will accomplish the goals you have today? Possibly not. Imagine that in five years' time, someone is going to give a speech about you to describe what you have accomplished in that time, and present you with an award for so doing. What would you like them to be saying? What would you like them to say you have accomplished? That will start to focus your mind on what you really want out of life. Take a moment now and think.

All successful people, in all walks of life, in all fields of endeavour and accomplishment, have goals. I remember once saying at an in-house seminar; 'I'm sure even sportsmen and women have their goals set, I'm sure that Nick Faldo, the world-famous golfer, would have set his goals, how else would he have achieved so much in his chosen field?' During one of the breaks in the seminar, a young man came up to me and said, 'I'm sure what you say is right for commercial situations, but I don't think golfers set goals, I bet Nick Faldo doesn't set goals.' I replied that I didn't really know, but that I would find out. Sure enough, I found out the name of Faldo's management company, rang them and spoke to his assistant. She didn't know either, but said she would find out. She did, he does. I had a fax letter back confirming that Nick Faldo does set goals, in writing. I'm absolutely certain, still, that most successful people set goals.

One of the stories so often told about goal-setting is the one about the class of 1952 at Harvard University. Evidently the class responded to a questionnaire asking if they had written goals for their lives. Just 3% had, 10% had goals which weren't written down, and the other 87% didn't have any goals at all. After 20 years, a follow-up questionnaire completed by the class of '52 indicated that the 3% that had written goals were worth, when added together, more than the 97% put together. This must tell us something. It confirms to me what I have always believed; that goal-setting really does pay off.

The power of 257

First, a piece of mental arithmetic for you. Imagine you are a tennis tournament organiser and have been asked to organise a tennis tournament – a singles knockout competition. Two hundred and fifty-seven people apply to play in the competition; you job is to find out how many matches, altogether, there will be. Two fifty-seven people, singles knockout competition, how many matches altogether?

Use the space provided, before you turn over the page.

→

The answer is quite simple; it is 256 matches. At the end of the day, there will only be one winner, that means there will be 256 losers. As, in singles knockout competition, everybody loses only once, to get 256 losers we need 256 matches. Well, how is that relevant to goal-setting?

If we look at where we want to get to, what is our destination, rather than the starting point, then the road there become obvious. I'm sure that if you had tried to work out the problem by starting at the front and having half play half and some go forward, it would have taken a great deal of time. However, looking from the back-end, in other words going into the future and looking back to today, made it easier. If we jump on a motorway without any thought as to our destination, we could as well end up in a northern city when we meant to arrive at a city in the south.

If it's so obvious to so many people that goal-setting is a good idea, how is it that many people don't set goals? Well, it might be some of these reasons:

1 They don't know how to set goals.
2 They fear failure.
3 They fear success.
4 They are too impatient to set goals.
5 Maybe they think their major goal is unattainable.
6 They fear rejection.
7 They don't make time or make wise use of their time to set goals.
8 They have self-limiting beliefs.
9 They think that goals are not important.
10 They have no ambition.

If we don't set goals, if we don't decide on the destinations we want to reach, how are we ever going to know if we have reached it?

Imagine for a moment that you had a magic wand and by lightly tapping yourself on the head with it you could suddenly be what you want to be. You could have the skills and, if appropriate, the money to be whatever you choose. The question is: 'What would it be?' Is there someone else in the world who is doing or being what you would like to be or do? Why isn't it you? Why isn't it you now?

When I am talking to people about goal-setting, one of the questions I often ask is: 'Who would like to win the lottery – even if you gave the money away after you had won it. Virtually everyone in the room puts up their hands. Then I say: 'Well, who does the lottery?' Eighty percent of the room usually put their hands down. By now you get the point: to win, you have to buy a ticket, just as in life. I call it The No-Lose Roulette Method; there is a way you can guarantee you don't lose at roulette . . . don't bet!

By the way, I'm not advocating gambling, you know exactly what I mean by these ideas. If you want to win the prize, you have to enter the race; goal-setting is the ticket. Some areas of life you could consider for setting goals include:

Time Goals, Career Goals, Education, Learning New Skills, Financial Goals, Fitness Goals, Community Care, Health, Personal Relationships, Leisure, Sports, Travel, Spiritual.

Some commercial areas you might look at include:

Learning to speak in public, keeping an ideas file, increasing your vocabulary, writing better letters, learning to read faster, learning to relax, learning how to sell, learning to negotiate, learning more about body language, learning how to release your creativity.

How to set goals

So, let's have a look how actually to set goals. It is really quite simple, but it will take time and, as I've said, I think that's probably the major reason why many people don't bother or else don't keep their goals up to date.

Set a time frame. Imagine that it is, say, five years from today. I've used five years, but you can use any time frame you want.

What would you have like to have achieved in that time? Write out a list in the space provided:

→

Now, go through those goals and, using the ideas shared with you earlier, decide which are 'A' goals, which are 'B' goals and which are 'C'; 'must do', 'like to do' and 'well, would be OK if I had the time'. Now think of a shorter time period, say one year, and do the same exercise in the space provided.

→

Again, prioritise them with 'A's, 'B's and 'C's'.

Do some of the goals on the one-year list lead you towards the five-year goals? Good.

We'll use what I call The Peter Principle, which stands for Precise, Exciting, Truthful, Effective action and Recordable. To make a goal reality, it must have these five points.

Precise. The goal must be precise, otherwise you will not know the correct enthusiastic action to take. For example, it's no good just saying: 'I want to be rich.' For a start, that's a future tense statement, which we will get onto in a moment, and second, what does rich mean? This is back to rules: we must have our own interpretation of the words. If you have a goal to be slimmer, that word slimmer or slim means nothing without some further definition and some exact weight. If you have a goal to be successful or happy, what is you interpretation of those words? The goal must be precise.

Exciting. The first 'E' in The Peter Principle. If the goal is not exciting, why bother to take action, let alone enthusiastic action? So make sure that you can generate some excitement at the thought, the anticipation of achieving the goal – or at least some pain at not achieving it.

Truthful. If you really believe that you can accomplish the goal and realise the dream, then it can happen. However, if you doubt that it is at all possible, you won't even try. For example, I'm sure it would be fun to fly to the moon under my own power on the 10th of September in the year 2020 – now that's precise, it's certainly exciting, but I don't think I'll ever be able to flap my arms fast enough to escape the Earth's gravitational pull, so it isn't truthful, so it won't happen.

Make the goals truthful.

Effective action. And what's more, *enthusiastic* effective action. If the goal does not involve you in taking action, then there is no action at all. No action, no feedback, no feedback, no result; and no result, no goal. We will discuss how to work out the actions in a moment.

Recordable. You'll need two record-keeping systems, because if you cannot record it, how will you know if you are on the right road and how will you know if you have arrived? So, the two record-keeping systems are simply those which tell you, first, that you are on the way and, second, that you have arrived.

For example, the way I do this is to use a sheet in the back of my Time Tracker, with a list of dates, dates by which certain things should have taken place. As I prepare my daily do-list, I check my goals to make sure I am taking the appropriate actions. If the goals need daily action, have a sheet of paper with a list of days of the month, an overview. As you take the actions each day, put a tick against the day; this catches you doing it right and there's nothing like that ever-growing list of ticks to motivate you to keep going.

Now write down your most important goal, ensuring that it goes along with the ideas of the PETER Principle:

→

The second part of the record-keeping system, then, is to tell you that you have arrived, that you have accomplished the goal and this is simply a remark made by you on the appropriate day in your planner. If that goal is some years away, put a note into your 1–31 file, so that when the day appears you can check that you have hit the goal.

So now you have a goal that is PETER: Precise, Exciting, Truthful, involving you in Effective action and is Recordable.

Next, as we discuss in Self-Talk, we must make sure that the goal is stated in the present tense and only in positive language. So, if the goal is to be worth a certain amount of money in so many years' time, you must write the goal as though it has already happened, because that sets up the pressure to perform the actions. You do that by using the statements: 'I am . . .', 'I do . . .', 'I have . . .' To reiterate: you must not use any future statements; if you say 'I will be . . .', then every time you say it, it hasn't happened; it's always going to be tomorrow; and, as we know, tomorrow never comes. So it must be 'I am . . .' This opens the filter on what is called The Reticular Activation System. Let me explain . . .

In our brains we have a filter, a filter that stops us consciously being aware of many things that are happening around us. The reason is that our conscious mind could not cope with all the information it could theoretically receive. For example, are you conscious of your breathing? Probably not until I asked the question and focused your conscious mind on it. We just take information into our subconscious and store it away, without being consciously aware of so much that is happening around us. However, when you say 'I am . . .', 'I do . . .' or 'I have . . .', then suddenly the filter opens for information pertaining to that situation.

For example, remember now back to the time when you were going to change your car. You hadn't perhaps thought of that car or certainly didn't notice particularly that make or model of car as you drove around. Now that you are focused on that car, now that you have decided to buy that car, that make, that model or even that colour, you suddenly see lots of them; everybody seems to be driving that car. Why? Because you've opened the filter. It's the same when you hear a word that you are intrigued by; you may have heard the word may times before and ignored it, but because you have become focused on the word, suddenly everybody seems to be using it.

So, by phrasing your goal in the present tense – 'I am . . .', 'I have . . .', 'I do . . .', particularly 'I am . . .' – you will notice the information and ideas relating to the goal that have probably been screaming past you for years and years, but were consciously ignored. You will be amazed. You've set a goal to take a vacation in a certain part of the world, suddenly you see advertisements for holidays to that destination. You set a goal to be a certain weight, suddenly you will receive information regarding a diet programme. You set a goal to have a certain handicap at golf, and someone will show you a new grip or technique that revolutionises your game. And all simply because you've opened the filter to allow the information to come in, to tell your conscious mind that this is the information you need.

We know that the phrasing must be in the positive; no linguistic negatives are allowed. The brain can't cope with 'I am a non-smoker' – it is getting 'I am a smoker – non.' It cannot make a picture of you not smoking without making a picture of you smoking. This is the same for all 'giving up' goals; you must focus on the new you, the solution, not the problem.

Third, the goal must make no sense. I know this sounds strange, but what I mean is that needs to be something that hasn't happened. If you set a goal to achieve something you have already achieved, then no pressure is created.

Now we're getting there. You have The Peter Principle goal, written in the present, positive tense. The brain, your brain, now knows what you want and knows the parameters you have decided upon. Next you must create the motivation to take action. To do that you ask yourself a question that will focus you on yourself and your surroundings and will focus on pain and gain – the two drives for action. The question is always one word . . . why?

Why do you want this goal to be accomplished?

Why do you want a million?

Why do you want to be happy?

Why do you want to travel to that exotic land, so far away?

Why? Why? and Why? again.

Until you answer this question, there will be no drive to take action, so you use the methods we have used before.

Write a number of pain paragraphs – paragraphs, mind you, not just words – and a number of gain:

Pain:

→

Gain:
→

Now that you have done that, you should be really tingling at the anticipation of accomplishing your goals. Now to the action you must take. Here are three simple methods:

1 Write anything that come to mind.
2 Use the Yesterday's Road Philosophy. This is based on one of the ideas discussed in Chapter 1, the idea that one of the most painful things that ever happens to us is to reach a point in our lives and think, 'If only I'd . . .', 'If only I'd done that'. Remember, I developed this when I had the problem of losing a major client and I asked the directors to imagine that we were in the future, hadn't accomplished the results that we wanted, and asked them to complete that crucial sentence; 'If only I'd . . .'

   So sit quietly for a moment and imagine that you have reached the date by which you have aimed to reach your goal and imagine that you have not reached the goal. Say to yourself, 'If only I'd . . . I would have accomplished my goal.' Then write down, in the space provided, whatever your mind tells you.

'If only I'd . . .

→

. . . I would have accomplished my goal.'

3 Imagine yourself in the future at the date when you should have accomplished the goal and . . . you've done it! Begin making the following statement to yourself and listen to whatever your brain tells you in order to complete it:
'I did it because I . . .' What are the dots?

If you still don't think you have all the answers, use the other techniques we've discussed. You could start with Role Models. Go and ask a number of people what actions they would take; however, be prepared to ignore their advice if that still-small voice inside you tells you they are wrong. They don't have your experiences, they can never know you as you know yourself.

When you have the goal using the Peter Principle, the Why questions, answers and actions, use the Salami Principle idea and the Carpet Fitter's technique to put the actions into the right order. Then sign that piece of paper, affirming that you will take the actions and you will take them enthusiastically.

If you choose to set goals with your partner, make sure that you do them separately and then compare notes. If you do them together, there's a chance that you or they will 'hedge your bets' – you might really want to accomplish one particular thing, but know your partner isn't keen. Just wait until you have been through the whole process and know where it falls in your priority list and then compare notes. It may be that you always wanted to go to the frozen north and your partner always wanted to go to the sunniest place on earth. If they are important goals, no doubt you can find a way to accomplish both; north one year, south another year. Do them on your own first.

Despite what many people say, I believe that it is not a good idea to share your goals with anyone unless they are totally supportive of you and your dreams. For unfortunately, so many people are negative in their Out-look and In-look, their Out-talk and In-talk, that they may dent your resolve: 'Huh, I don't know what you're thinking about wanting to do that' or similar sorts of language and attitude. Another reason is that people who are not into goal-setting believe that goals are only ever carved in stone, which isn't the case; sometimes the goal posts do move and maybe for a variety of reasons . . .

Imagine that you've changed your mind. Maybe through listening to the feedback from the action you've taken. Maybe inflation has changed your monetary goals. But for whatever reason, you've changed. Those negative people will give you feedback you just don't need: 'See, I told you that you wouldn't do it.' 'I knew you were aiming too high.' So don't tell them. Unless you have a person or people in your life who are 100% behind you and your dreams, aspirations or goals, just don't tell anyone.

Now to the steps:

1. Decide that you are going to give goal-setting a go, or, if you are already into goal-setting, that you will maintain your actions and update regularly.
2. Allocate chunks of time in your diary to do the goal-setting exercise.
3. Set one major goal.
4. Set one minor, short-term goal.
5. Do the 'Why' list.
6. Write the affirmations.
7. Visualise and, if appropriate, get pictures of the things you want to achieve.
8. Change your In-talk.
9. Set up a record-keeping system. Reading your goals at the start of every day is essential – how else can you take the right actions every day, unless you read your goals?
10. Record your affirmations tape.
11. Identify the possible obstacles that might prevent you achieving your goals – and decide how you are going to overcome them. Use the goal-setting method for all the goals you want to accomplish. You now have the technique, you can use it for anything.
12. Use the 'Crossing the Chasms' ideas for yourself and your people.
13. Be a 'goal-liver' as well as a goal-setter. If you think about prisoners who escape from jail, what always happens to them

within a few days of them escaping? That's right, they get caught and put back into prison. Why? Because they plan only to *become* free, they didn't plan to *be* free. When you are dealing with your goal-setting, don't plan only to accomplish, plan past the point of accomplishment also.

'Success is a journey, not a destination.'

Finally, think back for a moment to the people who are important to you in your life, the people whose respect and understanding mean something of value to you; perhaps your partner, children, parents, friends – and remember to include yourself. As the years pass by, what do these people expect from you? What do you expect from you? If you don't set these goals, what will be your situation or circumstances in life? Will you be living where you want to live? Will you be earning what you want to earn? Will you be as fit and healthy as you want to be? Will you have the relationships in your life that you want? What will people say about you? What will you be saying to yourself? Will you have accomplished your dreams? Will you be the role model for their dreams? Are they proud of you and your accomplishments? Only you know.

On the other hand, if you do get into goal-setting and the ideas we have discussed, what will these people be saying now? Will you be living where you want to live? Will you be taking holidays where you want to go? Will you be earning the amount of money you want to earn? Will you be fit and healthy and have good relationships? Will those people in your life who are important to you look up to you, and be using you as a role model for their dreams and aspirations? What will you be feeling? How will you look? What will you say to yourself? What does that reflection in the mirror say to you about the boss of Me Unlimited?

If you are into goal-setting, it says . . . Yes! Remember to take . . . enthusiastic action.

5 Financial management

Topics covered in this chapter include:

1 The importance of good financial planning and management.
2 The reasons why so many people don't have a home budget or financial management of any kind.
3 Simple ways to prepare a home budget (the benefits are enormous). For just a little effort, financial stress and worry can be reduced dramatically or even disappear.
4 Seven keys for solving financial problems.
5 The five rules for maximising your financial worth.
6 Looking at business budgets, including the golden rule that you should never break if you are in business.
7 In-talk programming: what we should say to ourselves about financial management.
8 The power of savings. You will be amazed, however good you are at mathematics, at the compounding effect of small, regular savings. How will you make those savings? By . . .
9 Negotiation. One major area of becoming financially secure is your ability to negotiate the price of items you buy, and so we look at eight ideas to enable you to do so confidently, 11 areas of planning negotiations, and seven manipulative techniques which others may try and use upon you.

All in all, some great ideas that will see you earning more and keeping more of what you earn.

The benefits

The major benefit of good financial planning is the relief of stress, which we have already touched on. Everyone says that, just like goal-setting, it is essential that we manage our own finances properly, and I'm sure most people would agree.

Imagine that, for a particular month, your salary, wages or income was reduced by, say, 25% – that you had only 75%, or three-quarters, of your normal income. How good would your financial planning be then? I am sure it would be very good, I know mine was, I've had it happen. Well, if we are forced to practise good financial management by simply imagining or experiencing living on just 75% of our income, why not do the same with 100% . . .

Speaking to so many people over the years about financial management, it seems to me that the percentage of people who have financial management in place is about the same as those who have goals. But that is not to say it is the same people.

We all have a good idea of how much we spend, often of how much comes in – but do we have written records? Do we budget so that we can enjoy more of the good things in life, the things we really want? Why is it that many people don't have their financial management in place? It think for much the same reasons as people don't set goals:

It would make things inflexible.
I like to live my life just for the moment.
I'm no good with figures.
My partner always takes care of those things.
My accountant is paid to do that.
I don't know how to do it.
Fear – all the usual varieties – and sometimes people are scared to find out just how bad the situation really is.
I don't seem to take (or make) the time to do financial planning.
I'm too busy living my life, running my business, keeping my job.

And yet financial management really is very simple to practise and actually a lot of fun. I know you may be thinking that I'm crazy: 'A lot of fun, Peter, doing financial planning? Maybe for accountants . . .' No, it *is* fun – and the benefits are enormous.

Just think: a feeling of being in control, and more money to spend. Yes, by not wasting money and by negotiating (with integrity) you can have more money. (Negotiation is a major skill we can, and ought, to teach children.) Financial management can mean a proper pension for our retirement; being able to save for that special occasion – a birthday or a wedding, perhaps; buying a special gift for someone you love; having something put by to stave off hard times – should they ever come – indeed, so many benefits, and yet it is said that many people at the age of 65 are either dead or dead broke. What will be your assets at the age of 65?

It's not what we earn or receive during our lives, it's what we do with it. For people who have worked 45 years, say from the age of 20 to 65, if their average earnings are just £22 000 a year, they will have seen a million pounds pass through their hands. Yes, that's right, a million pounds – just think of it . . . where did it go?

Some people believe that such things as setting goals and keeping records of their finances can make them inflexible. Well, I used to have that feeling too. However, I can guarantee that good financial management gives flexibility, it doesn't create rigidity.

Imagine this situation. There's an unexpected bill. Why is it unexpected? In most situations the unexpected is simply the unplanned. For people who have their financial records in place and know how much usually comes in and goes out, and who give some conscious thought to the likelihood of contingencies, it is likely that that which would be the unexpected for those who do *not* plan, will be the expected.

Take the major car bill; a new set of tyres, a new set of brakes, or the clutch – all *apparently* unexpected, but were they really unexpected? In most cases no. They weren't unexpected, they were unplanned. We know how many miles we are likely to travel in a year, we know roughly how many miles a good set of tyres will last and we can calculate the cost of the tyres – appropriately discounted, of course. So, not unexpected, simply not included in the plan. We know, at some stage, if we are responsible for the purchase of our own car then we are likely to have to replace that car; we can forecast the likely price we will get for our car on the second-hand market, and if we can't there are plenty of publications which can advise us. Thus we can allocate a portion of our savings to meet the expected (note I say the expected) cost. Most, though I agree not all, 'unexpected' financial situations can be catered for in our financial forecasting or budgeting. Just think of the major corporations or companies of the world; would the shareholders of those corporations accept from the board of directors that a major expense was not budgeted for or insured against? Of course not. So, let's accept that we are responsible for all our financial management. By doing so, we've already covered most of the potential problem areas and the reasons people give for not having a home or business budget.

Next problem. 'I don't have time, make or take the time for financial management.' Well, we've already covered time management and decided we do need to divide our available time into a variety of blocks or chunks, to make sure we are doing the things we want to do and not simply living to accomplish somebody else's dreams or goals. We agree that a percentage, however small, of our available time must be spent (and I repeat *must* be spent) on financial management. How? Simply by making an appointment with that most important person . . . you.

Imagine if your bank manager called you on the phone and said: 'I would like to schedule a meeting with you for just one hour at the end of the month.' Would you go? Possibly . . . probably . . . definitely? I am sure that for many people it would be probably or definitely. In that case, let's have the person requesting the interview be even more important than the bank manager. If the bank manager requested that your partner should also attend, would he or she go? Probably. Maybe there would be some conversation about 'What have you been spending on your credit card again?', or 'I told you not to buy that new suit, new car, new set of golf clubs (or whatever it was).' But the odds are that you and your partner will attend such a meeting.

Well, from that simple example we know that we can and would make the time, or take the time, to spend on our financial self-management – so much for time.

So what of those who claim 'I don't know how'? Well, from my research and personal experience, I have conceived a simple Financial Management System that will work for you. It is relevant, simple, easy, and not too time-consuming to use.

Profit and loss

In any business – and you of course work for Me Unlimited – there are two major areas to consider: first profit and loss, and second cashflow. Let's look at number one, profit and loss; it may seem that it doesn't apply to a private individual, but it does.

If you make a profit on your activities, and those activities may simply be attending the same place of work every day, then you'll have savings. Those are your profits. And, in time, those can be enormous, as explained below. If you spend more than you earn, then you will make a loss – and that might be an ever-increasing overdraft at the bank and the real reason for that call from the friendly, or not so friendly, bank manager.

We can make a profit in the same way any business makes a profit: we sell a product or service that is higher than the cost to produce it – quite simple. We sell our services to our employer, in an employed situation, or sell our services to our customers in a self-employed position . . . at a cost or price higher than the cost to produce the service. You increase the profits in the same way any company or corporation does; either by increasing the price at which you sell whatever it is you sell while at the same time keeping down the cost to produce the same. Or, by keeping the selling price the same and reducing the cost to produce. Or, if you are really good at this, by increasing the price at which you sell and reducing the cost at which you produce.

'That's all very well, Peter, but how do I increase the price of my service when I am on a fixed contract, or the market won't stand a higher price? How do I reduce the cost to produce when my mortgage and standard living expenses and costs are also fixed?' Good question, and one not easily answered with any certainty of increasing profits.

First, it will sometimes not be possible to increase prices or decrease costs, and in that situation you may well have to settle for what you get now, but you do have choice: stick with it if you're happy with what you're getting now, or change.

It can be the hardest thing to do if you are unhappy. There is no good being stuck in a job that does not meet your financial aspirations and causes you massive stress. In that situation, you must either change the aspirations or change the job. Change the goals and dreams or aspirations, or change the activity, job or occupation.

Let's return to the main point. If you wish to increase your profits, your savings, your disposable income, you must either increase your selling price or reduce your cost price, or a combination of the two. To calculate your current profitability, you need to know your incomings and outgoings. So, take a photocopy of pages 178–182; as will you see, they are headed incomings and outgoings. Using your memory and the list now shown, list all of your income and all of your outgoings

INCOMINGS

WAGE SLIPS

DIVIDEND CHEQUES

RECEIPTS

RENT

CHILD ALLOWANCE

PENSION

ANNUITIES

MATURING
ENDOWMENT POLICIES

OTHER INCOME

OUTGOINGS

MORTGAGE

GAS

ELECTRIC

WATER

RENT

BUILDING INSURANCE

BUILDING CONTENTS INSURANCE

MORTGAGE COVER

PERSONAL INSURANCE

ACCIDENT INSURANCE

MEDICAL INSURANCE

CAR INSURANCE

TELEPHONE COSTS

ASSOCIATION FEES

SPORTING MEMBERSHIPS

MOTORING ASSOCIATION FEES

NEWSPAPERS/MAGAZINES

CREDIT CARD PAYMENTS

INTEREST

BANK INTEREST AND CHARGES

MOTORING CHARGES, TAX

PETROL, OIL

REPAIRS, SERVICING, RENEWABLE PARTS (OR THE WHOLE CAR)

TAXATION, LOCAL AND NATIONAL TAXES

CHARGES, COUNCIL TAX

STATE TAX

MISCELLANEOUS

FOR SOMEONE WHO HAS CHILDREN, THERE WILL BE ADDITIONAL COSTS ASSOCIATED WITH

CLOTHES

POCKET MONEY

BIRTHDAYS

PRESENTS

SCHOOL FEES

NOW THERE ARE OTHER AREAS IN WHICH YOU SPEND MONEY ON YOURSELF OR YOUR PARTNER

PRESENTS

ENTERTAINING

HOUSEHOLD REPAIRS OR RENEWALS

HOME STATIONERY, COMPUTER COSTS

TV COSTS

LOAN REPAYMENTS, GOODS BOUGHT ON CREDIT

CLOTHES

HOLIDAYS

PERSONAL SERVICES SUCH AS DOCTORS, DENTISTS, HAIRDRESSERS

FOOD AND DRINK

LEARNING MATERIALS: BOOKS AND AUDIO TAPES

RECREATION

ACCOUNTANCY

LAWYERS' FEES

CHARITY

There is no need to worry about the order of these things at the moment, or the amounts, just do a list of all your possible sources of income and all your possible areas of expenditure or outgoings. Go through your bank statements, your paying-in book, your cheque book and your memory to make absolutely certain you have picked up everything for both categories.

So now you have two pages, one the list of outgoings and one the list of incomings. What you need to do next is to go through all the paperwork you have and find out how much you spend in each of these areas. It would be as well, until you are running your budget on a regular basis, to use just one month as the period. Write down how much was incurred beside each heading – note that I said incurred, not actually spent. By this I mean that if you pay the phone bill and the bill is a quarterly one, then you didn't incur all the expense in one month; you probably incurred one third of the bill each month, so put down only one third of the amount. If you have a yearly bill which you paid, you obviously didn't incur all of that cost in one month, you incurred only one-twelfth. This will be the same with all of the incomes, of course. What you are trying to establish is the actual amount of money coming in; the income that's relevant for that month and the actual amount of money it costs you each month . . . the outgoings. Deducting the outgoings from the incomings will clearly indicate the surplus or profit on a month. If many of your bills are quarterly, you may prefer to do a quarterly budget. Same procedure, using your records, bank books, paid bills etc., and calculating how much it costs you to run your life for the quarter and how much income comes in throughout a quarter.

This exercise is going to take you some time to complete, but it will be massively worthwhile – so do persevere.

Cashflow

Cashflow, as we know, is slightly different from profit and loss, analysing as it does when the money comes in and when it goes out. Now photocopy pages 185–7. As you will see, there are the same possibilities for headings as used in the profit and loss account, so again you will need to prepare for yourself and complete the appropriate headings on the pages. What we will do now is look at a three-month period.

INCOMINGS	**Month 1**	**Month 2**	**Month 3**
WAGE SLIPS			
DIVIDEND CHEQUES			
RECEIPTS			
RENT			
CHILD ALLOWANCE			
PENSION			
ANNUITIES			
MATURING			
ENDOWMENT POLICIES			
OTHER INCOME			

OUTGOINGS	**Month 1**	**Month 2**	**Month 3**
MORTGAGE			
GAS			
ELECTRIC			
WATER			
RENT			

INCOMINGS	Month 1	Month 2	Month 3
BUILDING INSURANCE			
CONTENTS INSURANCE			
MORTGAGE COVER			
PERSONAL INSURANCE			
ACCIDENT INSURANCE			
MEDICAL INSURANCE			
CAR INSURANCE			
TELEPHONE COSTS			
ASSOCIATION FEES			
SPORTING MEMBERSHIPS			
MOTORING ASSOCIATION FEES			
NEWSPAPERS/MAGAZINES			
CREDIT CARD PAYMENTS			
INTEREST			
BANK INTEREST AND CHARGES			
MOTORING CHARGES, TAX			
PETROL, OIL			
REPAIRS, SERVICING, RENEWABLE PARTS (OR THE WHOLE CAR)			

INCOMINGS	Month 1	Month 2	Month 3
LOCAL AND NATIONAL TAXATION			
CHARGES, COUNCIL TAX			
STATE TAX			
MISCELLANEOUS			

FOR SOMEONE WHO HAS CHILDREN, THERE WILL BE ADDITIONAL COSTS ASSOCIATED WITH

CLOTHES

POCKET MONEY

BIRTHDAYS

PRESENTS

SCHOOL FEES

NOW THERE ARE OTHER AREAS IN WHICH YOU SPEND MONEY ON YOURSELF OR YOUR PARTNER

PRESENTS

ENTERTAINING

HOUSEHOLD REPAIRS OR RENEWALS

HOME STATIONERY

TV COSTS

LOAN REPAYMENTS, GOODS BOUGHT ON CREDIT

INCOMINGS	Month 1	Month 2	Month 3
CLOTHES			
HOLIDAYS			
PERSONAL SERVICES EG DOCTORS, DENTISTS, HAIRDRESSERS			
FOOD AND DRINK			
LEARNING MATERIALS			
RECREATION			
ACCOUNTANCY			
LAWYERS' FEES			
CHARITY			

As you will see, there are three columns at the right-hand side of the headings. Now what you need to do is to put, under the month heading, when the money was actually spent, or received. Then, by adding up the expenditure columns in each month and by adding up the income columns in each month, you will know if your cashflow is positive or negative; more cash in than out, or more cash out than in. As you continue to analyse the cashflow for a longer period, you will clearly see if you arrive at a point of positive cashflow, or if there are periods of negative cashflow, when you will need additional funds to meet the bills – an overdraft or a loan.

Many businesses which get into financial difficulty don't do so because they are not profitable. They may be extremely profitable; often they can get into difficulty because of their cashflow; they have made their sales but the money and profits from those sales haven't come in as fast as they wish them to. They have to pay their suppliers before the customers pay them, they have to pay wages and all the other usual business expenses, before they get their hands on their own money.

If the situation for such businesses is that the owners or directors are unable to put their hands on sufficient cashflow from their own resources or with borrowed money, such as bank overdraft and loans, the business will be trading past its capital base and go bust. This is all common sense. However, many small businesses do not have cashflow and profit and loss analysis and forecasting in place. They know that they are profitable because they have a good feel for the business and they cannot understand why they are experiencing financial difficulties; and of course, as their sales improve, the problem gets worse. Financial planning is essential for everybody. So do prepare for yourself, for all the areas of your life, some simple financial analyses of profit and loss and cashflow, if you don't already do so. Actually knowing what is happening with your money is the start to any financial management. You will be able to draw your own conclusions from your analysis as to the actions that you must take to ensure profit and positive cashflow.

And so to the Golden Rule of business:

'Pay yourself first'

Now I know that this may seem fairly obvious, but in so many businesses it simply isn't the case. Many owners of small and not-so-small concerns have personal overdrafts which really should be part of the company's overdraft. By paying yourself first, I don't mean don't pay the creditors or your staff, but I do mean pay yourself first. If the business can afford to pay only staff and the creditors, so that you get merely any little bit that's left and thus keep expanding your personal overdraft, it's time to take a good, hard look at that business. If it's not capable of making a profit . . . your salary . . . why are you doing it? The day of reckoning will surely come.

Maximising your financial net worth

It is often said that money is the root of all evil. The complete expression is:

'The love of money is the root of all evil.'

Money itself isn't evil or bad – it's the use to which it's put. We can put our money to good use. We can feed and clothe ourselves and our families. We can give to charities and needy causes. We can put money back into the system by spending money on the things we wish to buy. Like it or not, it's a commercial world and money is the medium of exchange.

Let's look first at the seven keys:

1 Skill improvement. Always be on the lookout to improve the skills that you will be able to use profitably. (See the knowledge-gathering plan, including personal development of skills, in Chapter 4.)
2 Savings. Put a percentage of your income, however small, into savings. It's amazing how much it can mount up to. We go through this in detail below.
3 Make money. Think of money-making activities as hobbies rather than work, it's surprising how many of them can make money. This again is not to say you have to become fixated with making money . . . quite the opposite! If money-making is a hobby, it's the doing that's the fun – money is just the result.
4 Think carefully. Make sure that you think carefully before you spend. Do those budgets, know what your cashflow and profitability situation is.
5 Insurance. Make sure that you have sufficient insurance – insurance for home, people, cars, etc.
6 Pensions. Have a pension plan of some description – you don't want to end up dead or dead broke at 65. The sooner you start a pension plan, the cheaper it will be.
7 Investments. Your home can be a marvellous investment, so check that mortgage you have on it, if you have one, is the right one for you. Circumstances do change and what was right when you bought the house may not be right now. For many people, their house is the largest single purchase they ever make. Be aware and keep up-to-date with the mortgage market.

Now the five rules for maximising your net worth:

1. Pay yourself first. Put by a portion of your money each month for you, or in other words, exactly the same as any business owner or director, pay yourself first.
2. Take care. Be careful if you are offered any schemes that offer incredible rates of interest. Yes, there are such schemes that can pay off, but often very high interest rates can involve higher risks. This is not to say you should be negative about things – just be careful.
3. The experts. Consult the experts and learn from them, there are many excellent money advisers who have the appropriate experience. However, as I have said before, you must learn all you can for yourself so you can judge the advice given by experts.
4. Knowledge. Don't put your money into a business you don't understand. Find out about the people running the business. What is their experience? Have they run successful businesses before?
5. Venture capital. This is the field of venture capitalists who know that a certain number of businesses will fail. If you are a venture capitalist, that's great, you know the risks. If all your savings are risked on just one business and you don't know the business, perhaps that's the wrong investment.

Make certain, by investigating the papers and money journals, that your money is getting the best rate of interest it can, while still meeting the risks you are prepared to take. You can divide your savings into a number of areas: first, absolutely no risk; secondly, still safe but a small risk; and thirdly, slightly riskier but a higher rate. It's your money – you have to decide what you want.

In-talk out-talk programming

We now need to look at in-talk out-talk programming, on the words you have been saying in order to programme your mind in relation to money. Some people say such things as: 'I'll never earn enough money to pay off this mortgage.' Others: 'Why do bills always come now?' Those in control of their money and that programme say: 'I'm a money-making machine', 'I'm in control of my finances', and 'I love to do budgets'. Remember, enthusiasm for the subject makes it easier to understand, and remember also to programme what you want.

Savings

Let's now consider the power of savings. We will, for the sake of ease, and allowing for inflation, if necessary, assume that you earn £50 000 per year over a ten-year period. In that time, you will earn half-a-million pounds, over 20 years one million pounds, 30 years one and half million, and 40 years two million.

Imagine if you could save just 10% that's £50 000 after ten years, rising to £200 000 over 40 years. Perhaps 10% is too high; at 5% that's still £100 000 over 40 years. If you were able to put that 5% into savings (the 5% you are going to save by negotiation), what could it amount to? Well, 5% would be just £6.85 per day, let's say £5 a day.

For the sake of this discourse, we will assume that your savings are split into three areas: no risk, some risk and high risk, and that you average over those risk areas and over the year 12% interest. Now you may think that this is high or low, depending on your current knowledge about investment and when you are reading this book, but I'll assume 12%. Just £5 saved, per day, monthly, at 12% interest over ten years, would be £35 334. Over 20 years, £151 950, over thirty years £536 841, and over 40 years a staggering £1 807 000.

Well . . . where will this £5 a day come from? Negotiation; as well as wherever else you decide. If £5 a day sounds high, let's put it in perspective. Going back over ten or 20 years, inflation running at, say, between 3 and 7% reduced the real value of money in the earnings of most of us by half every ten years. So our £5 a day was only £2.42 a day ten years ago and a mere £1.17 a day 20 years ago.

However, if £5 a day is too high in your current circumstances, let's start at a smaller figure, say £2.50 a day, increasing in ten years' time to £5 a day and increasing in another ten years to £10 a day. Now let's reduce the overall interest rate in the three risk areas to 10%. At the end of ten years, £2.50 a day, saved monthly at 10% per annum, would give you £15 706. At the end of 20 years (remember, you have now increased to just £5 a day for these last ten years and you still have £15 706 to start with), it would have grown to £73 929. At the end of 30 years, another ten years with increased savings of £10 a day for the last ten years, it would have grown to a staggering £262 955, that's just £2.50 per day for ten years, £5 a day for ten years and £10 a day for ten years.

If you could cope with just £5 a day for 30 years, at 10% it would still have come to £346 647. It has to be worthwhile looking at your saving goals. At negotiating your investment stake.

Negotiations

I've always found that most things in life are negotiable. However, many people don't negotiate the price of things they buy. The reason, I think, is the usual fears coming into play, particularly the fear of embarrassment, and yet so often when people are away from their own surroundings on holiday, particularly in abroad, they are quite happy to negotiate or barter in the local market, having fun with the traders, putting on mock frowns or smiles and walking away with the purchase discounted, as happy as can be, no embarrassment, no fear.

If people can do it abroad, why not at home? After all, *abroad* is only home for someone else. Perhaps it's also because people don't know what to say, or how to negotiate. I am sure the following ideas will help, focusing on how important each little negotiation is to your overall accomplishment.

Just ask. The first way is quite simple and very very obvious . . . just ask! How much is this item? What price will you do this at? This will often have people discount the price. It's fairly easy to say and if you have any problems, remember that confidence is simply the application of confidence and there is nothing like practice and preview review to set up situations in your favour. Practise the lines before you go into any negotiation.

Someone else. Second, imagine that someone else has asked you to buy the item in question, such as your partner, and they have told you the limit you can spend. You will hear people selling things from home saying: 'My wife says I couldn't accept less than . . .' You can use the same idea, 'My partner says I mustn't spend more than . . .', or 'The boss has told me that X is the most we can spend.' Usually, the situation is that someone else is concerned in how much is spent. You might use: 'My partner goes mad if I don't get discounts when I'm buying. How much shall I tell him I paid for this?'

The Golden Rule. The Golden Rule of many negotiators is:

> ***'Never accept the first offer.'***

For example, you ask for a discount in a shop – by the way, all negotiations, in my opinion, should be carried out in a friendly win-win manner; frowning gets nothing but refusals. A smile and a light tone of voice will work wonders. So you ask for a discount, and you get the response: 'I could give you 5%.' You know as well as I do that it is very rare for someone to give their best offer immediately. Perhaps a slight hesitation on your part and, 'Well, I was looking for more than that, what's the *best* you can do?' will see further discount obtained.

I know that when you go to put in a bid on a house that you want to buy, you never start with your best offer. Other people are just the same.

Imagine that you go to buy a car from a second-hand car sales operation and, having picked the one you would like to buy, you make a ridiculously low offer for the car – way behind what you would really pay, for you are just testing the water. The car salesperson responds with, 'OK. It's yours.' How would you feel? 'What's wrong with it?' 'What have I done?'

So often it isn't the price, it's how we arrive at the price that makes everyone feel that it is win-win, so if you accept someone's first offer, you haven't given them the satisfaction of haggling. They feel the conversation has come to an end too soon. Enjoy the conversations of negotiation; most people do like to haggle.

Next, a question you can ask in all sorts of situations to find out if negotiation is possible: a simple 'Do you have the authority to give discounts?' Most people give an honest answer to this question, and if they do have the authority they answer 'Yes', in which case it would be pretty poor financial management not to ask for how much discount you can have. However, if the answer is 'No', simply ask, 'Who does have the authority?' and then ask to see that person. When the person arrives, check the situation: 'I understand you have the authority to give discounts, is that right?' The 'Yes' you know you will receive will again see you easily asking how much discount you can have.

We touched earlier on the idea of the power of questions within the Subconscious Encoding Process and you know from that brief discussion that people usually answer questions that are asked, even if they do not verbalise the answers.

A question that you might use in shopping could be: 'I'd like to look at . . . [whatever it is]; however, I never pay retail – that's OK isn't it?' The 'Yes' answer lets you know that discount is available and we owe it to ourselves to spend the right amount of money.

My basic philosophy behind all this is twofold. First, most shops have sales: January Sales, Winter Sales, Spring Sales, Autumn Sales, you name it. Some shops seem to have a permanent sale. If the shop is happy to sell me the same product in the sale at a certain price, they why wouldn't they be happy to sell it to me now at the same price? I'm not trying to cheat the shop or store in any way; I am just looking for the sale price they would sell it at anyway, albeit at a different time.

Second, with most companies, most goods carry an amount of bad debt provision built into the price. Any company that offers credit in any way will have a bad debt provision. If I am going to pay the bill now and not create any bad debt, I don't see why I should have to pay for the people who don't pay. You understand my thoughts on this . . . I'm not asking for all the company's profits – far from it; I want the companies I deal with to be profitable, have a good cashflow, still to be there in years to come so I can deal with them again. However, if I am paying on the day, that takes care of my part of the bargain with cashflow. If I am paying at all, that takes care of my part of the bargain on bad debt; they don't have any as far as I am concerned.

Always trade. 'Always trade, never concede' is a well-known expression in negotiation, meaning that if you give way on some factor in the negotiation, it's only right and fair that the other party gives way in return. In selling, it might be that you reduce your price in response to a request for a lower price, but only for a six-month contract to supply. You might paint the goods in the customer's colours, but only if they order 200 of them. I'm certain you can personalise this.

The power of 'If'. This brings us on to the most powerful word in selling and negotiation and trading and conceding: the word 'If'. If we are able to make our statements conditional on other things happening, we haven't committed ourselves. For example, 'If you give me an order for six items, then I will do . . .', 'If you give me X price on these, then I will buy ten'. It is always 'If you do it, I will do it' not 'If I do it, will you do it?' The latter way takes the decision out of your hands, the former keeps the decision in your hands. So the system must be 'If you . . ., I will . . .'

A variation on the idea of asking someone if they have the authority to give discount can be used when dealing with intermediaries or agents. Quite simply, express your preference to deal with the principal. For example, 'I would prefer to deal with the owner on this matter, because I like to deal with the person or persons who have the authority to negotiate' will quickly establish whether the agent or intermediary has the power to negotiate the deal.

Experiments have shown that most people respond to certain words in certain ways. The particular words I am thinking of are: 'I need . . . because.' When we say to someone 'I need [whatever it is] . . . because . . .', they are more likely to respond positively to those words than many other forms. For example, 'I need a discount because my partner says I have to have one', 'I need to have six of these at this price because . . .' (and whatever reason you can think of). Research indicates that the words after the word 'because' are actually of little relevance; it seems not to matter what is said, it is the 'I need . . . because' which creates the favourable response.
Let's examine the steps of negotiation:

1 First, do your research, particularly in commercial situations. Find out all you can about the company or people with whom you are to negotiate.
2 Define your goals before the meeting. What is your best outcome? What is the worst situation you will accept? What is your realistic expectation?
3 Walk in their shoes. By that I mean take a moment and go through all of the steps listed here as though you were the other person looking at you.
4 Calculate the real cost of any concessions you might make.
5 Always make notes during the meeting.
6 Have an agenda.
7 Plan your questions in advance and practise them.
8 Listen actively.
9 Use 'We' and not 'You and I'. Aim for that win-win.
10 Avoiding blaming or threats, scoring points or insults and shouting. Be careful with the language you use and avoid the use of 'but' – it is confrontational; use 'and' or 'however'.

Manipulation. Let's now look at the range of manipulative behaviour people use on us, or try to use on us, in negotiation.

1 *Authority*
In this form of manipulation, people will tell you that they have the authority to buy or sell at the start of the conversation, and then say they have to check with someone else at the end of the conversation. To avoid this, ask precise questions at the start and watch carefully to see and hear if the other person is telling you the truth. Perhaps at the end of the conversation remind the person of what he or she said at the start.

2 *The Russian Front*
Some negotiators try to use what is called 'The Russian Front'. They say that certain factors in the discussion are not negotiable. That may, I repeat may, be the truth; however, don't take it as read.

3 *The Mother Hubbard Technique*
This is when someone says the cupboard is bare, though they may not use the actual word 'cupboard'. In commerce they use the word 'budget', as in 'We don't have that figure in the budget'. It may be that another budget could be used. I have seen people in marketplaces put the exact amount of money they wanted to pay for the item in one pocket and put the rest of their money in another pocket and then, having taken out the amount that they wanted to pay, they show the market trader their empty pocket lining and said, 'That's it, that's all I have.' People do this commercially, they just use the word 'budget', but it's still the Mother Hubbard Technique.

4 *The Two Hats*
This is a method used by police forces the world over and by car salespeople and others. One man wears the black hat – he's the hard one; the other man wears the white hat – he's the soft one. The soft one appears to be on your side and calms down the proposals or questions of the hard one. It seems acceptable to believe what the soft one says. To deal with it, tell them that you understand the method they are using and that, in future, you will take what each says as if they had both said it.

5 *The Salami Principle*
The Salami Principle of negotiation is rather like the Salami Principle for avoiding procrastination – a piece at a time. Having agreed on an arrangement, some people would chip and chip and chip in the hopes of moving you a bit further – just resist if the deal has been struck.

6 *Power Plays*
Why do large companies have large receptions with flowers and the glorious smell of coffee? Why does the boss have a large desk, higher than the lowly visitor's chair? Power plays is why – games to make you feel that negotiation isn't possible. To avoid them, treat everyone as you would wish to be treated, treat everyone as equal.

7 *Perceptions*
Sometimes our own perceptions of situations hinder rather than help us. If we believe that someone is more important, we mis-perceive our chances. For example, you apply for a job and have been asked to attend for an interview at the company's premises at, say, 10 am. You arrive at 9.50 and there in reception are 20 people, similar to you, about the same age, dressed in the same way, sitting nervously. How have your chances of getting the job changed? Have they gone down? No.

I forgot to tell you that the other people already work there. Sometimes we mis-perceive situations; never assume.

These are the common manipulations which work against us, either by the design of others or by our own perceptions. Be aware of them and you will improve your chances of negotiating everything.

So let's move on to the main steps of financial management:

1 If you have not previously done a home budget, recognise why. This is self-management. Or if you have previously done one, but not kept it up to date, why not?
2 Do a home budget using the broad brush, simple method

which I have described. You will be amazed at how good you feel.

3 Go through the seven keys for financial problem-solving and the five rules for maximising your financial worth and take action with them.
4 If you are in business, decide now to obey the Golden Rule: *pay yourself first.*
5 Reprogramme your new and enhanced skills of Financial Management: 'I am a person who regularly does financial planning. I am in control of my finances.'
6 If you haven't already got one, start a savings account. Make a note now in your do-list for today or tomorrow and give it 'A' priority.
7 Decide now that you can and will negotiate more and more.
8 Use the methods I have outlined, practise with them on friends, family and colleagues, until you are consciously confident and subconsciously competent in their use.

All of these skills will make you richer than you will be if you don't use them, and you can utilise that additional wealth and lack of financial pressure to accomplish more of your dreams and goals, but if, and only if, you use these skills, perhaps better stated as . . . take enthusiastic action.

6 Mind and brain

In this chapter, we look at two fascinating areas: first, the mind and brain; and secondly, creativity. We examine how a better understanding of the mind and brain will help you in your aim for more accomplishment.

We'll start with memory, how it works, explain an excellent way of dealing with the multiplitude of information that comes your way, give keys to memory and describe a system that you will be able to use immediately to increase your memory – perhaps better stated as 'increase your recall'. Then a second system for memory recall, and eight tips to help you remember more. Next we examine the brain, the conscious and subconscious mind, provide a proven system to enhance skills, and explain the power of questions and how you can use them to access immense creativity and your own information storage system, as well as how to use them to persuade others. Then we will touch on autogenics and the learning systems of Giorgio Lazanov, followed by three exercises for the eyes and help with rapid reading. Next, how to have a knowledge-gathering plan – after all, if we increase our knowledge and then use that knowledge, we must be able to accomplish more. After that, a simple technique to relieve minor aches and pains using your mind, a six-step process, how to conquer nerves, the jigsaw approach to learning and reading, and the steps to take to increase or enhance skills in all of these areas.

Memory

The first topic we are going to examine in this fascinating area of the mind and brain is the memory. Some scientists now say that the hippocampus, which is an area near the centre of the brain, is responsible for mapping and organising the memory and directing certain of those memories to different parts of the brain.

There are a variety of theories as to why our memories work. One is the small electrical charges which trigger various activities; another, that chemical pathways are formed; and yet another suggests that we have memory molecules or complete memory cells. In operations where the neo-cortex – that's the grey outermost area of the brain – is stimulated with extremely mild electrical currents, people experience a flood of memories; sights, smells, sounds of their past, so vivid as to be truly outstanding and yet . . . nobody has so far come up with the definitive answer as to how our memories are created and subsequently recalled.

The Russian psychologist, Alexander Luria, discovered in the 1920s that a journalist named Solomon Sherevsheuski, had nigh-on total recall. 'S', as he was later to become known, seemed to be able to remember everything, seemed to have all of his senses working in harmony, and would describe the feel of red or the look of emotions. He could recall every word from conversations he had had many years previously. However, this became a problem to him, as you can imagine. One difficulty was that he used to struggle to recall voices and faces, he simply said they changed too much. I'm sure that the constant bombardment of our conscious mind, caused by almost total recall, would reduce us – as it did 'S' – to being merely a performer of memory feats, rather than someone with an ability which would enhance everyday living and accomplishment.

We often hear the expression, 'photographic memory', and it is true that some people do seem to have such a memory – what is called an eidetic memory. Leonardo da Vinci could draw an incredible likeness of somebody after just one meeting. Napoleon Bonaparte had the same skill with maps. It is certainly true that improvement of our memory recall can have positive spin-off effects in so many areas of our lives.

One of the easiest memory systems I have ever come across is the system developed by Dr Bruno First. I saw an advertisement in a Sunday paper over 25 years ago and sent for it. I still have it – a series of blue books in a now battered cardboard outer. Let me share the basic idea with you; I am certain you will find it fun and extremely useful.

The system is based on what has been termed 'Memory Hooks'. I have researched many systems that have used this idea. By being able to link new information, via a memory hook, to information that is readily accessible in our minds, we create a simple but powerful system of recall of that new information. So, to start with, we create a main list, a main database, which can can be used for all the hook procedures. We allocate a word for each of the numbers one to nine, and for nought, those words being as below:

1	Tea
2	Noah
3	May
4	Ray
5	Law
6	Jaw
7	Key
8	Fee
9	Pea
0	The sound is Sh or Zz

Go through the list and lock the words and numbers into your mind. When I first read and saw this explanation, I thought the ideas were crazy, but go through it and I know that you will come to the same conclusion that I did. The ideas do work.

1 Tea
Now an easy way to remember this is that the capital letter T has one stroke down – we always ignore the vowels in this system, so a straight line down for the capital letter T easily reminds us of: 1 is Tea.

2 Noah
A capital N has two straight lines down, so: 2 is Noah.

3 May
Again ignoring the vowels (we'll use the 'y' as a vowel in this situation), a capital M has three straight lines down, so we can easily remember that: 3 is May.

4 Ray
This is slightly more difficult, this is the ray, as in a ray of sunshine or the ray of a torchbeam. Now you can imagine with a torchbeam that it actually has a figure four in its shape. You can imagine a point at the top, coming from the light itself, spreading out, making a kind of V shape. If you draw a line across the V, then you will make the figure four. As I said, some of these ideas do seem strange to start with, but they will work. So: 4 is Ray.

5 Law
You can imagine a policeman putting up his hand with four fingers and a thumb; that will remind you that: 5 is Law.

6 Jaw
If you look at someone in profile, you will see the figure six in the shape underneath their chin, coming round towards their lips – there is a six shape with their chin in that way so: 6 is Jaw.

7 Key
Again ignoring the E and the Y. If you can image a seven as a key, using perhaps a brass seven to undo a lock. 7 is Key.

8 Fee
The way in which I remember this is if you squash the eight, it makes it look like a pound sign. 8 is Fee.

9 Pea
If we take a capital P and turn it round, we will have a nine – that's a simple way to remember it. 9 is Pea.

0 The sound of Sh or Zz – and that you will simply remember.

So the list again is:

1	Tea
2	Noah
3	May
4	Ray
5	Law
6	Jaw
7	Key
8	Fee
9	Pea
0	The sound Sh or Zz

Next, let us add a list that we wish to remember by linking or hooking the new information to the list that you have now created in your mind. With but a few minutes' practice, you will easily remember the main list – but if at this stage you can't, work back through it until you can.

The list we are going to add will be:

Table
Chair
Television
Mouse
Car
Dog
Golf ball
Briefcase

Plate
Boat

We are able to associate or hook the new list to the main list because we tend to remember things that are unusual, and also things which involve movement, more easily than everyday static objects. When hooking the new list, make sure that the picture you create is unusual and moving. This is how to do it:

1 Item one was Table, so we have to associate a table with Tea. In your mind, think of or create a picture of a large cup of tea, enormous, let's say two metres across. Then, again in your mind, pick up the table and throw it into the cup of tea, so that it makes a massive splash. Now that's an unusual picture, and in future you will immediately be able to think of number one, followed by our keyword tea, followed by the word table.
2 The keyword is Noah and we want to associate the next word on our list, which is the word Chair. Let's imagine that we have a small chair and a large Noah, the large Noah sits on the small chair, breaks it and falls to the ground. That's a picture we can easily recall. So, number two equals Noah equals chair.
3 The word on the new list is Television. We know that the keyword is the word May and I like to think of this as a maypole, with coloured streamers spinning round and then put the item I want on the end of those streamers. For example, in this situation, put televisions on the end of the streamers and we can see them spinning round and round and round. We might even think of some of the televisions coming off the streamers and crashing to the ground.

Now let's just recap:

Number one: keyword Tea, associated word Table
Number two: keyword Noah, associated word Chair
Number three: keyword May, associated word Television.

You can see how simple this is. Now what I would like you to do is to go through and link the words from the new list onto the keyword listing as follows:

Number four: keyword Ray, associate with Mouse
Number five: keyword Law, associate with Car
Number six: keyword Jaw, associate with Dog
Number seven: keyword Key, associate with Golf ball
Number eight: keyword Fee, associate with Briefcase
Number nine: keyword Pea, associate with Plate
Number ten: keyword Toes (0 represents the sound Ssss or Zzzz, 1 is tea, 10 is therefore tea+Ssss/Zzzz so we will use the word Toes), associate with Boat

Now that you have made your unusual and moving associations, let's see how well you got on. Here is the list of the numbers with the keywords; check if you can remember the list linked to it (it is listed together on the next page):

1	Tea
2	Noah
3	May
4	Ray
5	Law
6	Jaw
7	Key
8	Fee
9	Pea
10	Toes

1	Tea	Table
2	Noah	Chair
3	May	Television
4	Ray	Mouse
5	Law	Car
6	Jaw	Dog
7	Key	Golf ball
8	Fee	Briefcase
9	Pea	Plate
10	Toes	Boat

The way in which you can expand the system is to create longer lists to use for numbers over ten. This is done by linking the numbers together by sounds. The sounds are as follows and they work on the basis of the English language:

1 The keyword was Tea, but you can also use D.
6 The keyword is Jaw, but you can also use the sound CH, which is very similar to Jaw (CH as in Choice).
7 The keyword is key, but you can also use the hard C sound, such as the C in Cash.
8 The keyword is Fee, but you can also use Vee.
9 The keyword is Pea, but you can also use Bee. (As you can hear and see, the sounds are extremely similar.)

Now let us say we want a hook word for our main list where the number is 11. Well, we know that the letter for one is T, so 11 is two Ts. Because we don't concern ourselves with vowels (they don't count in this system) we could make the word TOT. The word we could use for number 20 would again be made out of N as in Noah and the sound Ss as in zero, so it would be NS or the word NOSE.

Thirty-seven could be MACK, M which is three and K which is seven. The beauty of the whole system is that you will be able to remember the items inside out or in any order. For example, what number was table? That's right, number one. When we thought of table, the picture of the table splashing in the teacup came to mind and from there to one was easy. What number was television? That's right, three. Again, go through the list and make sure that you know the main word list and practise associating different words to it.

Now let's examine how we can deal with incoming information more easily. For example, to write out every single word in this book would take a number of hours, as you can probably imagine. Most people, when they take notes, take them in a linear format; that is to say, straight down the page. However, I'm sure you can remember back at school, when you had a diagram to label and you had notes all over the place. For example, a diagram of the human body, with labels for arms and legs etc.

We are able to make use of the way in which our brains prefer to receive information, i.e. pictures, colours and keywords, by using the Mindmapping ideas originated by Tony Buzan. I've seen similar ideas, such as Dan Lee Dimke's random access notes and even now computer programs using the same idea of Mindmapping.

Let's say, for example, that you are at a seminar or meeting. In the centre of your notes page, which is far better as a blank sheet rather than lined paper, with the paper in landscape, rather than portrait position, draw a colourful picture representing the theme of the meeting. Then, as the meeting progresses, just add keywords, notes and pictures from lines from the central image. The reason this works so well over and above linear notes is that you hop about all over the page: you might start off down one line and expand it, adding other ideas and drawing rather like a road system [creating a road system-like drawing], including new pictures. Then start a new line in a different direction from the central image. Suddenly a piece of information comes along that has more relevance to your first line and it is easy to add it there. With linear notes, it is very difficult to add bits of information into the lines.

You can use this idea for preparing speeches, for taking notes from TV, radio or audio programmes, from books, or for preparing a report. If you are going to prepare a speech or report, start with a central image and add legs and ideas, notes and pictures, wherever they are appropriate. As the 'Road

System' builds, you will see that you have written groups of relevant information together.

What I then do, with my notes, is to take a thick-tipped felt pen and draw round the various groups; then you can decide in which order you wish to present the groups. It really does work so well.

I used Mindmapping to prepare my original notes for my audio programme 'Accomplishment, The Science and Practice', which is the basis of this book.

Try the idea for yourself and see how it works.

The five keys for memory

1 **Unusual.** We tend to remember things that are unusual; if you were to look out of your window now and saw a medium height man in a dark suit with dark hair, carrying a briefcase, you would probably have forgotten him in a few seconds. However, a seven foot tall man, dressed in a bright red suit, with trousers that are too short, showing his pale green socks, carrying a miniature parasol in black, with large white spots on it, could probably be described in 20 years' time. As already noted, things that are unusual stick in our minds.

2 **Linking.** If we are able to hook or link information to things we already know, it will create great recall, as we found out with our ten items.

3 & 4 **First and lasts.** We tend to remember the first thing that happens in any situation and we easily remember the last thing that happens in any situation. This is called Primacy and Immediacy. For example, can you remember your first date? Can you remember your first day at your current place of work? I'm sure those answers were 'Yes'.

Can you remember your last date, or your last meal, or your last day at work? The answer again – 'Yes'.

We tend to remember firsts and lasts and have difficulty, at times, with the things in-between – this is called Memory

Sag. When you hold meetings, they should not exceed 45 minutes to one hour before taking a break. If you are studying or working on anything that requires memory, take a break every 45 minutes or so, to let your brain have a rest and assemble the information you have already input.

5 **Repetition.** If you repeat information on a regular basis, it will move from your short-term to your long-term memory. Having received information, it is a good idea to repeat or review the information ten minutes later, then the next day, then one week later, then a month later, and then at regular intervals thereafter. It will then stick.

The beauty of Mindmapping is that you will be able to review a whole seminar or a day at a meeting within a few seconds; whereas plowing through pages of notes is both time-consuming and difficult for your brain.

Action. Another aid to memory is, believe it or not, taking action. It is said that we remember about 5% of what we hear, 25% of what we see, and 90% of what we do. You'll be able to relate to this; you go to ride a bike, many years after you originally learnt, with no practice in-between, and within a few seconds you can ride quite easily; only a couple of wobbles and away you go. If, one summer holiday, you stand at the end of the swimming pool, having not been swimming since the previous holiday, you do not ask yourself, 'Can I still swim?' – you know you can, because you know you remember actions.

Feedback. When we practise our motor skills, sports skills or manual skills, we need to have feedback. Practice or repetition of these types of skills without feedback is very hard work. Imagine hitting golf balls in the dark; would you get better? Not as quickly as you would if you could see the results; there is no reinforcement of what does work and no discarding of what doesn't, if there is no feedback. With all practice, take action, check the feedback and see if the action was the right action.

Additional ideas to improve memory recall include:

The House Dash Method. This is a memory hook idea. Imagine if you were to walk around your house, in and out of certain rooms, and remember where, say, five objects were in the room: the TV, the kettle, the bed, the bath, the wardrobe. Five objects in each room, I'm sure you can easily do that, try it for yourself. Now, in you mind, go around twice as fast, then ten times as fast. It's pretty easy to do, isn't it? If before you went at speed, you had linked or hooked by unusual pictures with actions, a list of items, one by one, to the items you have picked out in the rooms, then as you were speeding round (ten times faster), those items would still be hooked there. Try this for yourself; it's another excellent system of memory hooks.

Enthusiasm. Being enthusiastic about a subject improves memory recall. Just wanting to recall things enables us to recall them. You'll know this with children; they may not be able to remember all their homework details, or even what they had for lunch at school, but they can name every character and every attribute of those characters from their favourite TV programme. Why? Because they have enthusiasm for the subject.

Attention. If you pay attention by active listening and active watching, you will get better memories and make it easier to recall. Have you ever noticed how singers are able to sing in a language they cannot speak; they just remember the tune of the words. That's how most of us learn our tables.

Acronyms. Use acronyms – words made up of the starting letters of a series of words, such as HOMES for the names of the great lakes, Huron Ontario Michigan Erie Superior. Use nonsense things, as in how to remember the colours of the rainbow: Richard Of York Gave Battle In Vain (Red Orange Yellow Green Blue Indigo Violet).

Blocks. It is also helpful to keep information in blocks; the brain likes blocks. Mindmapping helps with that. Sir John

Gielgud, the famous actor, said that he always found it easier to remember a whole play, rather than bits of it.

Enjoy puzzles . . . stretch yourself.

It has been said by many scientists that we use, at best, only 5% of our brain's capacity. Just think, if we could expand that to 6% that would be a 20% increase. Just 10% would be double; what could that mean for your accomplishment potential?

The brain is divided into two main parts: the left and right hemispheres. The left side, for most people, controls such things as logic, language, numbers and scientific concepts. The right controls patterns or shapes and artistic imagery. It was often thought that the right brain was the creative side – but scientists are now saying that both sides can be creative.

The conscious and subconscious mind

Although there are one or two dissenting voices, it is generally agreed that we do have a conscious and subconscious mind.

The conscious mind. The conscious mind is the screen of our computer; it's the area into which we call information from our database – our subconscious mind. With information on the screen, we get the opportunity to evaluate that information, to accept it or reject it.

The subconscious mind. The subconscious mind doesn't judge, it just deals with information – hence the success of In-talk programming. It goes straight to the subconscious for processing.

Some researches say that, at night, the brain rebuilds itself and sorts out the information that it has received during the day. This idea is obviously backed by those well-known expressions we touched on earlier. Maybe that's why subliminals work; they are bypassing the conscious and going straight into the subconscious, where no evaluation takes place, no judging, just information storage. Affirmations are obviously based on the same idea.

There is extensive research that says that the brain cannot distinguish between something that has actually happened and something that has been vividly imagined, hence the success of such experiments with skills training, where two groups of people are asked to practise in two distinct ways. One group actually practise the skill, one group simply imagine that they are practising the skills. The result: a remarkably similar increase in ability. Try it for yourself and see what results you obtain. I have used the idea in a number of areas of self-development and am convinced of its power.

Our conscious mind tends to hold only one thought at a time, hence the idea of positive Out-look and positive Out-talk. If we are thinking or speaking positively, that's the state we will be in.

We have touched on one of the areas of the Subconscious Encoding Process, the power of questions. Now I'll explain how this power can be utilised to work for you.

When a question is asked, be it a self-question, perhaps using our self-management questioning methods, or a question asked by another person, there is no choice about answering; the process just takes place. For example, 'What colour are your eyes?' If you know the answer without looking in a mirror, the answer just pops into your mind. It is extremely difficult, if not impossible, to resist. That's why I call it the power of questions.

When a question is asked your subconscious database is opened and the answer brought to the front screen, your conscious mind. This is how we use the self-management questions: by asking the questions, properly phrased and as specific as possible, the subconscious will give you an answer – all you have to do is listen. If you have the answer, your subconscious will find it. Sometimes you have to give the subconscious time to sift the information, for if you try to force the answer, you sometimes cannot find it. You have a word on the tip of your tongue and strive, in vain, to recall that piece of information, using your conscious mind, but the information isn't stored there. However, as soon as you let go, off goes the system and the word pops out of your head. This is why self-questioning is such a powerful method.

Visualisation

We described forms of visualisation and the Lazanov techniques for learning in Chapter 2. Now let's consider the idea of Autogenic Training. Autogenic means self-produced, but the expression 'Autogenic' has become associated with relaxed learning.

As already mentioned, studies have shown that relaxed visualisation of a successful action can enhance performance. Major athletes and sports people in many countries use this method, actually visualising the successful outcome of their event, seeing the whole race or competition in their mind's eye, with some remarkable results – remember Nick Faldo, for one. Relaxation seems to be the key; it is the relaxed state that enables access to the subconscious, so let's look at some relaxation techniques.

IF YOU WOULD LIKE TO RECEIVE A **FREE** BONUS TAPE, INCLUDING SOME RELAXATION EXERCISES, PLEASE WRITE TO ME AT THE ADDRESS SHOWN AT THE BACK OF THE BOOK.

The first method of relaxation is to tense all of the muscles in your body for a count of ten and then relax, let go completely – and then repeat the exercise. Try it now. Tighten all of the muscles, starting with your feet, moving up to the legs, now the lower body, now the chest, your arms and finally your head, all of the muscles tense. Hold for the count of ten, now relax completely, let everything go for the count of ten. Then do again two more times.

The second way to create relaxation is visualisation. Simply imagine yourself in a relaxing place of your choice and create a switch word which will take you to that place and anchor.

The eyes

Let's move on now and examine the eyes, the only part of the brain that is visible. Here are some eye exercises you can use to strengthen your eyes and improve visual tension. The first we have discussed already, so I won't dwell on it: visualising a scene for a second or two and then looking away, before trying to bring back the image.

The second exercise is to focus on something very close to you (by close I mean a few centimetres), say a pen or your finger, and then, without moving your eyes from side to side, to focus on something in the distance. This exercise, focusing on something near and then on something far, each for only a second or so, should be done for only a minute at a time in total, to avoid straining the eyes. The effect is an increase in the strength of the muscle that focuses the eye.

Researchers report that people who have worn glasses for a number of years have been able to do without those glasses after persevering with this exercise.

The third exercise is Holding Positions. Sit upright in your chair, or stand upright, head held erect, but not stiff. Now look in the following directions, each for no more than 30 seconds at a time, again to avoid strain . . . (If there is any strain at all with any of these exercises, reduce the amount of time until your eyes build up their strength.) . . . the areas to look at are: Up-Right, Up-Left, Down-Right, Down-Left, Side-Right, and Side-Left. You may also add: looking down with your eyes closed, as though you were trying to look at your tongue, or – again with your eyes closed – looking upwards at the spot between your eyebrows, about 30 seconds in each direction.

All of these exercises can strengthen the eyes and reports indicate some remarkable effects, such as enhanced memory and enhanced creativity.

Knowledge-gathering plan

As we are currently using only about 5% of our brain's capacity, it would be as well to have a knowledge-gathering plan as part of our curriculum. As we are learning, we often go through a four-stage process: from subconscious incompetence, to conscious incompetence, to conscious competence, to subconscious competence. Let me elaborate. We start at the subconscious incompetence level; in other words we don't know that we don't know. Take driving a car.

Before we could ever drive, we did not know that we did not know how to do it, it probably looked easy. Then came the first time that we tried to do it and realised that we didn't know – that is conscious incompetence; we know that we don't know. After we've learnt to drive for a while, and still much of the time today, we are consciously competent; we know that we know and we use the skills.

Next comes the stage where you have been driving for a while and suddenly you cannot remember the last few miles; you were on 'autopilot', you had become subconsciously competent.

We need to move all of our skills into these top two areas: consciously competent (we know that we know) and subconsciously competent (we just do it without even knowing we are doing it). So it's a good idea to have a knowledge-gathering plan, to be hungry for knowledge. You will be amazed at how much people know. Feed your mind with information, use the power of questions and your active listening skills. I believe we can never overload our mind.

You might look at rapid reading, having a better vocabulary – one study indicated that there is a direct correlation between people's vocabulary (and their use of it) and their position in the commercial world:

higher vocabulary – higher position
lower vocabulary – lower position

it seems to make sense.

You could set a goal to look up five new words a day – that would be over 1800 new words per year. Think how that would help with creativity and communication skills.

You might consider improving your vision, using the eye exercises I have outlined. You might decide to increase your manual skills – learning to juggle, learning to write with your other hand, learning to write with both hands at the same time – why?

Why not?

If you have the time and the inclination, nothing is impossible. Leonardo da Vinci used to draw pictures with one hand, while making notes about the diagrams with the other. Sir Edward Lanseer, the 19th-century British artist, used to amuse dinner guests by drawing a horse with one hand and a stag with the other . . . at the same time! If they can do it, well . . .

All of these ideas could be included in the personal development section of your goal-setting. If you have decided to improve a particular skill, remember it usually gets worse before it gets better. For example, let's say you can type with just two fingers, and then you learn to type using all your fingers – your speed will probably decrease for a while, but then move on in leaps and bounds. You might change your golf grip – your game will get worse before it gets better, but it will get better provided the grip is the right one for you. It will also bring you to heights of accomplishment that the old skill would never have enabled you to reach.

It is the same with all skills: be prepared for a slight downturn in some areas before improving to the skill level that you always wanted for yourself.

Relieving minor aches and pains

Here is a system that utilises the brain to relieve minor aches and pains. When, for example, you have a headache, use the power of questions, of the Subconscious Encoding Process. Ask yourself the following questions: What shape is the pain? What colour is it? What smell does it have? How does it feel? What does it sound like? What does it taste like? Keep coming up with answers, however crazy the answers are, for those six questions, again and again and again, and you will find the pain will disappear.

The Superman method. And now a technique to take feelings from one part of your life to another part of your life. Imagine that you have to give a presentation to a group of people, and you are feeling nervous about the event. Sit quietly and relax, and bring to mind an occasion from the past where you felt totally confident, so confident that you could see what was happening around you, hear what was happening, feel exactly what you were feeling. Really re-live that experience of being totally confident in yourself and your abilities.

Now imagine that you are in a telephone booth, the type used by Superman to change from Clark Kent into his alter ego. The telephone booth has just grown out of the ground around you. In your mind, open the door of the booth and step out, leaving those confident feelings inside the telephone booth. Keep stepping away from the booth until you know that you have left all of the confident feelings inside it.

Now, in your mind, go forward to the time when you have to give the presentation. Picture the scene, what you'll be seeing, what you'll be hearing when you get to the part when you are announced to speak, or just about to enter the room. Put the telephone booth in the picture, open the door and step into the booth and feel all those confident feelings again. Now open the door, step out with all those confident feelings, as invincible as Superman. Well, that's it, you've programmed those feelings for that occasion in the future.

You can use this method, the Superman method, to take any feeling from the past and programme it into the future. Try it – it's simple, it's easy, and it really does work.

The Jigsaw Approach

Finally in this chapter, before the steps, let's cover the Jigsaw Approach to learning. This again was developed by Tony Buzan. It's such a simple idea, but so effective.

If you have to read a book or report, treat it in the way in which you would treat a jigsaw. Find the corners first and then add in the edges until the picture is rather like a frame; then work in the pieces, sometimes one at a time, sometimes a number together. When you come to a hard piece, something that won't fit in, what do you do? You see that it won't fit, so you put it to one side, totally confident that it will eventually fall into place.

The same approach can be used with a book or report. Take an overview of the book to get the idea of what the author is going to discuss or cover – that's the corners. Look down the chapter headings and any illustrations, any summaries and the index – that's the straight edges. Then start to fill in the jigsaw by reading anywhere in the book that takes your fancy. If you come to a part that you don't understand, skip it – it will no doubt fit in later.

This really is a great way to speed up learning, and having used the idea regularly I can confirm that it also creates a better understanding of the material. It may be, with some books, that a look at the summaries of each chapter would be a good idea; I've had occasions when I have read the summaries and then had no need to read the book.

Now to the steps:

1 Practise with the memory hooks number system until you can do at least 20 items in and out. It's a great party trick.
2 Begin now to use Mindmapping, or Random Access Notes.
3 Plan your meetings to allow for breaks.
4 Set up a feedback system for all of your practice.
5 With all incoming information, take action to make sure that it moves from your short-term to long-term memory.
6 Create acronyms, acrostics or rhymes for important information you need to remember.

7 When you need a solution to a particularly knotty problem, use the night method of asking yourself a question before you go to bed.
8 Spend some time working on the questions you will ask yourself and others – use the power of questions.
9 Learn to listen to and trust your inner voice, what has been called 'The Silent Witness'.
10 Do your In-talk programming about your mind, brain and memory learning skills: 'I am a person with a superb memory recall', 'I always remember faces and names', 'As I get older, my memory gets better and better'.
11 Practise visualisation of the successful outcome of the events in your life and use the Preview Review Technique for all important meetings.
12 Get more information on Super Learning, or try as I did with a baroque music tape with large tempo music, learning new words from a foreign language.
13 Practise relaxation every day (send for your free bonus tape).
14 Do the eye exercises, long and short focus and eye positions.
15 Decide on your own knowledge-gathering plan. Spend some of that precious commodity – time – and prepare a list of the things you would like to learn. Then, using the systems we have discussed in our goal-setting section, set the goals, prepare the plan, take the actions, check the feedback, keep records. Include learning new words.
16 The next time you have a minor pain, headache or the like, try the pain relief six-stage method.
17 Use the Superman method to move past feelings into the future.
18 The next time you have a book or report to read, use the Jigsaw Approach, allied to Mindmapping, and prove to yourself it really does work.
19 Because we have covered so much in this chapter, read it again.

Although we've covered a great deal of information, we haven't even begun to scratch the surface of mind, brain and learning. If this area fascinates you as much as it fascinates me, take steps to find out more. The use of the various skills we have discussed in this chapter will have an impact in all the areas of your life, because you take your brain, your mind, and your ability to learn with you everywhere. Use them or lose them. I know you will use them by taking . . . enthusiastic action.

Creativity

Now to one of my favourite topics . . . creativity. How can you be more creative in all the areas of your life? Let's start by doing two tests, to see just how creative you currently are. Then I am going to share with you ten different methods to release your creative juices and get them flowing so fast you will wonder how you will get the time to use all the ideas you generate. Finally, six steps to take to prepare your own Enthusiastic Action Plan.

The brain. As already mentioned, the old idea was that the right brain was responsible for creative thought, but researchers now believe that the left brain can also play a part. The old idea was that the left brain was responsible for logic and language, that it was the dominant side of the brain. Now it is believed that the right brain is dominant. The reality is that we have two sides that are able to work together to produce creative ideas.

The problems associated with people being creative can frequently be traced back to school. Often, we were taught by linear method, by rote, by correct answers only – and yet of course all inventions started with someone having a thought, and a thought that was frequently outside the normal rules of what could, or what should, happen in any given set of circumstances.

When the first automobiles were on the street, there was a man in front with a red flag, not only to warn pedestrians of the oncoming menace, but also to ensure the car didn't go too fast; it was always thought that our hearts would explode from our bodies if we went at speeds which today we regard as slow.

People jeered at the idea of the printing press, the plane, the size of boats we have today, and even sailing around the world.

The attitude which seems to have prevailed with all great inventors and creative people is that there are no failures, only results, only lessons that can be learnt. Charles Kettering, a famous American inventor, once remarked: 'From the time a child starts kindergarten to the time he or she graduates from college, he will be tested two, three or even four times a year. If he fails once, he is out. An inventor may fail nine hundred and ninety-nine times and succeed just once and he is in. An inventor treats his failures like practice shots.' What a great philosophy to have, what a great attitude.

Edison claimed, when asked how he coped with so many failures in his attempt to perfect the electric light bulb, that they were not failures, just steps along the way – another great attitude.

The founder of IBM, Thomas J. Watson, used to say 'The way to succeed is to double your failure rate', and the Nobel Prize winner, Linus Pauling, said that the secret in coming up with good ideas was to think of as many ideas as possible and just get rid of the bad ones. The sum total of all of these peoples' attitudes is that there are no failures. Release your creativity and learn from every attempt.

Now some creativity quizzes:

1 As a mark out of 100, how creative do you believe you are?

→

2 Have you ever been in a traffic jam and found your way by some back road, so that you arrived at your destination more or less on time?

→

3 Have you ever decorated a room, or picked the carpets and curtains for a room?

→

4 Did you decide what to wear today?

→

5 Have you ever painted a picture in your life?

→

6 Have you ever taken a photograph and decide where you wanted the people to stand, or decided that you wanted a particular leaf to stick in the corner to make an artistic effect?

→

7 Have you ever designed a letterhead or a form of any description?

→

8 Have you ever planned the way to get somewhere?

→

9 Have you ever planned a party or a social gathering?

→

10 Do you understand that it is what you believe, in other words how good you believe you are, that determines how good you are?

→

11 Do you understand that if you believe you are creative . . . you are creative?

→

All of the preceding questions were about creativity – finding your way around a traffic jam, decorating a room, deciding what to wear, painting pictures, taking photographs – and I would imagine that you were able to answer 'Yes' to most of them. Let me ask you another question:

As a mark out of one hundred, how creative are you?

→

Let's move on to the second test, which designed to measure creativity. It begins with the name of an everyday item, and what I want you to do is to take two minutes only to write down or think of as many uses for that object as you can.

Paperclip

→

Using this test for many years, I have found that the average number of answers was four. If you had four, well done, if you had eight, very good indeed. If you had 12, excellent. If you had 16 then you are certainly in the ranks of the most creative people around.

Now that we have proved to ourselves from these two tests that we can be creative, and so can most people to a variety of different degrees, how is it that people don't use that creativity? First, I think that many people's In-talk Out-talk programming has been, 'I am not creative', 'I am hopeless at solving problems', 'It's just not me'. Well, to correct that we just change the programme. I think the other answer is probably that some people don't have some simple systems to use and I am going to correct that situation now, with the following ten methods:

1 The Einstein Method. It has been said that Einstein came up with the Theory of Relativity when he was just daydreaming; he was sitting on a grassy bank and he imagined he was riding a sunbeam. His thoughts on that idea started his investigations into relativity. We can use this idea. Many famous people – inventors, researchers, scientists, business people, academics – say that time spent daydreaming is time well spent. I agree.

We sometimes daydream when we drive – we are subconsciously competent. We can daydream in the bath or the shower or while taking a walk on the beach or in the countryside. Take the time to let your mind wander from the activities of day-to-day living; let it go and who knows what theories and ideas you will come up with during those times.

2 The Reverse method. This is where we take a problem or difficulty we have and simply turn it on its head. For example, one way I used this idea was to ask the directors and managers in my company: 'How can we pay the sales force less money?' They thought it was a strange question. However, by coming at the problem from a different direction, they began to see different solutions. When I received the answers, I just turned the ideas around – and had numerous ways to pay the sales force in my company . . . *more* money. If we were paying the sales force more money, chances are that they were making more sales; that's what I was after.

Edward de Bono, the man responsible for the expression 'Lateral Thinking', was, according to a story I heard, once employed by a major American police force as a consultant, to come up with ideas to decrease crime. He turned the problem on its head and suggested that all the people were made police officers; from that, Neighbourhood Watch was born.

'How can I make less sales?', 'How can I be less successful?', 'How can I earn less money this year?', 'How can I have less time to do the things I want to do?' There are so many ways to use the idea.

It can relate to home life as well as business life. 'How can I spend less time with my family?', 'How can I increase my golf handicap?' Just let your mind wander and answer the questions for you. We know how the Subconscious Encoding Process deals with questions. Well, let the answers come out; just empty your mind onto paper and the turn the answers around.

3 The Dictionary Idea. This again is based on a story I heard about Edward de Bono. I understand that he was asked by a major Japanese TV manufacturer to come up with a new concept for a television set.

Opening a dictionary, he stabbed in his finger and found the nearest noun. It happened to be 'cheese'. Now, the way to use this is to try to associate the word 'cheese' with the problem or opportunity in hand. How can we associate 'cheese' with TV? Well, perhaps we could have 'smellivision' – maybe a scratch-card provided for cookery programmes. No? Oh well, could we have TV which is cheese-shaped, cheese-coloured? What about holes, holes is a good idea, what could we use the holes for? Holes for speakers? Holes to keep the remote control? No, OK, what about a hole in the screen to see what happens inside a TV? With modern-day electronics, that would be pretty boring, wouldn't it? But what about a hole in the screen to see what's on the other channels? That's it, that's exactly what de Bono came up with, a hole in the screen to see what is happening on other channels, a picture within a picture, available today – and all from the word 'cheese'.

You and I can use that idea. Simply get the idea you are working on or playing with within your mind, open the dictionary at any page, stab in your finger and find the nearest noun. Now associate that noun with a problem or opportunity. By taking your mind off in a different direction, by looking at the problem from outside the usual linear mode, it's amazing how many strange and wonderful ideas your mind will provide. Just try it.

4 Dare to be Different. This idea is so simple, it really is that . . . dare to be different. Often, people come up with ideas and then don't have sufficient belief in them to give them a try. Let's just do it . . . to see what happens, provided we have calculated the possible downsides and know what the risks are, in both time and money. If those risks are acceptable, just dare to do it.

I once heard a story of a man who was in the life insurance business and he was suffering from a problem of people not wanting to talk to him. At social gatherings, when talk got around to 'What do you do?', he would answer, 'I sell life insurance.' People would back away with a polite smile on their faces, 'Oh, I see, nice to meet you', and quickly get into conversation with someone else, because of the fear that as a life insurance salesman, he would be trying to sell them something.

So – he dared to be different. He decided to change just one word in his four-word response of 'I sell life insurance', replacing 'sell' with 'buy'. Then, when people asked him, 'What do you do?', he would respond, 'I *buy* life insurance.' 'You buy life insurance, what do you mean?' 'Well,' he would say, 'I go to the insurance marketplace for my clients and I look for the exact type of insurance that they want and I buy it for them. Would you like me to buy some for you?'

What a great idea. I used to use it when we were selling money as a leasing brokerage. I would say to people as a response to the question, 'What do you do?', 'I buy money.' You can imagine what an excellent start to a conversation that was. Think of how you might use the idea.

I once heard a story about two frogs. It was an excellent attitude story and I decided it would make a great idea for a mailing piece, a mailshot. We sent out audio tapes, about ten minutes long, advertising our seminars. The tape was entitled,

'Once upon a time there were two frogs . . .' The response was fabulous. Not many directors of companies get a mailshot on audio cassette and even less with such an unusual title as 'Once upon a time there were two frogs . . .' Sometimes it pays to be different, so dare to be different.

5 The Nightingale Method. I call this The Nightingale Method after the famous American presenter, Earl Nightingale. It is one of the simplest ideas to use and also employs the power of questions. Earl's method was as follows.

Simply write out, at the top of a piece of paper, a question to yourself, such as 'How can I make better use of my time?', 'How can I make more money?', 'How can I improve whatever situation or skill I want to improve?', and then force yourself to write 20 answers – it must be *20*. I know from experience that the first ten are usually easy, but then it gets a little harder and you begin to think that 20 would be impossible. However, persevere, because I have always found that once I'm past the 14 or 15 mark, my 'second wind' comes along and sometimes 30 answers are written and I am still going strong.

My suggestion to you is that you do this for three days running, after all it only takes about 15 minutes at the most to do, and after three days you would have 60 new ideas for whatever problem or opportunity you were thinking about.

In my in-house seminars, when dealing with creative problem-solving, I've had a room full of people from the same company or department write 20 ideas each before the next coffee break. Hundreds of ideas are generated in only a few minutes, even allowing for the overlap of ideas. When you use this method, don't worry if some of the answers are crazy; just like the 'cheese' example I gave you, sometimes taking our mind off in another direction really can help.

6 Visualisation. We have discussed visualisation and the various ways in which people visualise. Allied to the Yesterday's Road philosophy in our goal-setting section, visualisation techniques can be really powerful. All you need to do is visualise yourself past the point at which you wish to have accomplished something, and imagine you haven't. You then say to yourself, 'If only I'd . . ., I would have done it,' and then wait for your mind to tell you what those dots are. Or the positive way: 'I have accomplished this because I . . .' and again listen to what your mind says. It is so simple to use.

7 The 'What if . . .' Method. If you can get into the habit of asking 'What if . . .' questions, then you will open up your creativity. Imagine you are in a rut at work . . .

'A rut is only a grave with the ends kicked out.'

Things are going along OK, but nothing exciting is happening and you are not particularly happy with the amount of money you earn. Try asking yourself 'What if . . .' questions. 'What if we did it this way?', 'What if we didn't do that task at all?', 'What if I poured a can of blue paint over the chairman's head at 11.06 tomorrow morning?'

Dare to be different, dare to ask yourself crazy questions. Who know where it may lead you mind, your brain, your creative skills. And tied to that 'What if . . .' question is the 'Why' question. 'Why do we do it this way?', 'What if we did it that way?' 'Why?', 'Why?', 'Why?'

Sometimes, situations just evolve. That is not to say that they are always right, but everything does change.

8 The Sleep Method. If you are struggling to come up with an answer to a particular situation or problem, tell yourself the problem last thing at night and then ask your mind to come up with an answer by morning. Remember the power of questions. So many people throughout history have said that they have gone to sleep with a problem, only to be awakened with the solution and all the necessary details. Try it for yourself. I suggest that if you do try this idea, that you keep a pen and pad by the side of the bed so that the moment you wake, you can write down whatever your mind tells you.

9 The Windows of Opportunity.

A
B
C
D
E

1 2 3 4 5 6 7

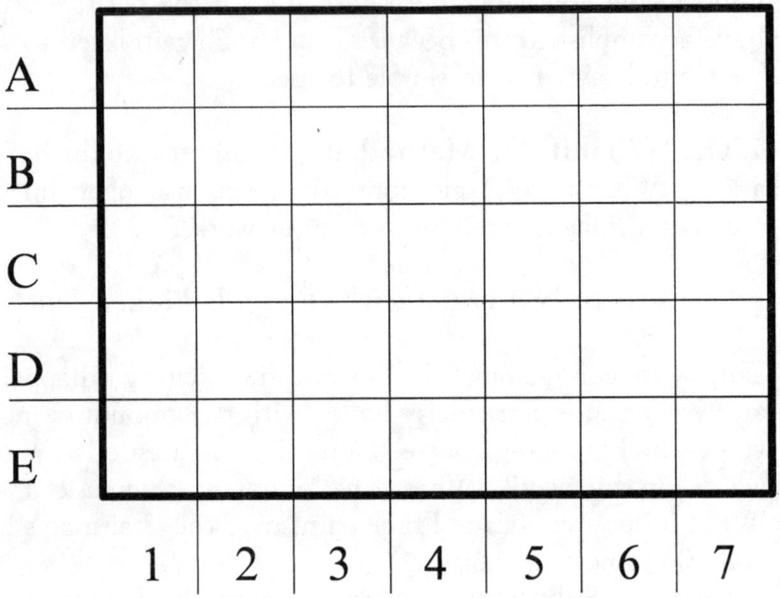

As you can see, this is rather like a chessboard. This is how you use it. If you are in business and want to increase the number of products that each of your customers buys, then down the left-hand side of the diagram you would label 'A' through to 'H' as the names of your customers; and across the bottom, '1' through to '8', as the names of your products and services. Where the squares meet, you would colour in that square if that customer buys that product or service. With a large customer list, or a long list of product, you could prepare this on a spreadsheet programme on a computer. The holes that are left uncoloured, I call the Windows of Opportunity; there is an opportunity to sell that product to that customer.

It is often said that it costs about seven times more to sell a product to a new customer as it does to sell a product to a current customer or client. I know that it is necessary to keep 'topping up' our original business, by selling to new customers.

However, what about the customers who we already know, who already buy from us, who already know our payment terms, already know our personnel, what about them? Do they buy the whole of our product range? Has anyone ever asked them to buy?

This focusing creative exercise, because that's what it is, can have fantastic results.

The Windows of Opportunity form could also be used to focus your mind on the activities you might wish to carry out with family members. For example, down the left-hand side of the diagram put the family members' names, and along the bottom of the diagram the various activities. As each one is completed, colour in the squares. Children love to be involved in this type of thing.

A scoutmaster might use the idea to keep track of those who had taken and passed tests. A training officer might use it to keep track of those requiring tuition in certain skills. It can have so many uses.

10 Mindmapping. The way to use Mindmapping for creative problem-solving is to put a picture of the problem or situation you have in mind in the centre of the page, and then start the lines coming from the picture, going in a variety of directions. Keep adding information as it springs to mind. Find new information from other sources – books, tapes, people – and add this, too. Pretty soon a whole picture will begin to form which will, in many cases, lead you to a solution, or creative ideas.

All of the above methods have their devotees. I use Mindmapping, Visualisation, 'If only . . .' and the Twenty Answer method, more than any others. Try all of them to find out which ones suit you best. They can be used for so many different areas:

1 Increasing sales, and, thinking back to the section on Financial Management, increasing sales includes everyone.
2 Decreasing costs.
3 Increasing time availability.

4 Increasing the amount that gets done each hour.
5 Improving relationships.
6 Having fun.
7 Finding opportunities: commercial opportunities, social opportunities; vocational and vacational.

We can use these methods:

1 To solve problems, and to overcome writer's block if we have to write a report or letters.
2 To have creative sessions with the people involved in our lives.
3 To help others release their creative skills.

And so to the steps:

1 Use the ten methods I have described, at least once for each one, to find out which one(s) might suit your preferred style.
2 If you want to increase your product knowledge or wish the people in your company to have greater product knowledge, do a Product Knowledge Quiz. For example, have each member of a team bring five questions with five answers, hand those in to the manager (or whoever is running the meeting) and, if you have ten people in that team, suddenly you have a 50-question test. *Note*: Everybody must get five right, because they brought the questions . . . and answers.
3 Do the Paperclip Test again, but perhaps with different items – a golf ball, a piece of string, a table leg, a sheet of brown paper, a knife – and try it in reverse: 'What couldn't I use a paperclip for?'
4 Programme your In-talk: 'I am creative', 'I am a creative person'.
5 Improve your memory by using the methods I have described, because increased recall helps creativity.
6 Have brainstorming sessions at work, perhaps using the Twenty Answer method. I really enjoy coming up with creative solutions and I know you will too. As always, use the information as soon as you can, or in other words, take . . . enthusiastic action.

Summary

So, let's summarise the vast amount of information we have covered on our journey to Accomplishment. The great thing about books is that you are able to re-read them at any time. Some research says that it is necessary to read messages at least 21 times before the information moves to your long-term memory.

We now have a number of ways to be more creative, ways actually to release the ideas that are already in our minds. We can relieve any stress created by money worries, by being at least totally aware of our financial situation. In the running of the business Me Unlimited, we have decide to pay ourselves first.

Please, I urge you, if you have not been into the idea of goal-setting before, or perhaps if you have not updated your goals as often as you might, set one goal and work diligently towards it. I just know it will work for you. You can now have at least one hour extra, every day, to use as you see fit, using the variety of ideas we discussed on Self-Management and Time Management . . . just by getting up one hour earlier for one week. Why not try it and see what happens?

You can overcome fear, break the chains and decide on your own rules for life.

You have a greater understanding of how the brain and the mind deals with information.

You now know that to accomplish anything at all – to have a result – you need to take action, that your actions are determined by your feelings, your feelings are created by your attitude, that your attitudes are created and determined by your beliefs, and that the beliefs are created by your In-talk Out-talk programming.

It's been great sharing my ideas with you. I look forward to sharing more of my ideas and thoughts with you as the years go by.

If you decide to use the information in this book, if you decide that you are the head of Me Unlimited, and if you decide to be the best you can be, I know that you will accomplish whatever you want, every single day of your life by taking . . .

ENTHUSIASTIC ACTION!

From me, Peter Thomson, for now . . . Goodbye.

Free Audio Tape

Side A of the free audio tape is divided into two parts. The first is called 'Good Morning', the second 'Good Evening'. In the 'Good Morning' section, I will remind you of some of the important things we have been through and of the fun we can have at the start of our day. In the 'Good Evening' section, I will simply share with you some ideas to finish the day, particularly a working day, so that by the time you arrive home, you have let go and filed the information of the working hours into the correct parts of your brain and mind. In that way you can relax and undertake whatever social activity you may have planned.

Side B of the tape is the relaxing part. You will hear some calming music and together we will take a brief journey that lets you relax totally and clear your mind. This side, side B, should not be played while you are driving your car or operating any machinery of any kind. I have designed it for you to use while you are sitting or lying down and able to take just ten minutes off from the activities of the day. You can use it as many times as you like during the day. If you are out and about in your car, you can play it at lunchtime, while you are parked. You can play it in the evening, or even when you have gone to bed. If you find you fall asleep, don't worry, that's OK. Use side B, the relaxing side, as often as you can.

Before listening to side B, decide on a switch word, to put you into a relaxed state of mind, because during the tape I will ask you to repeat that word mentally. It would be preferable to have word with three syllables, such as 'relaxing' or 'harmony' or something similar.

TO OBTAIN YOUR COPY OF THE FREE TAPE, SIMPLY WRITE TO ME AT THE ADDRESS AT THE BACK OF THE BOOK.

Index

'Now . . . take the next step!'

Now that you are using the proven ideas of the Pinnacle Principle it's time for you to take the next step.

'The Achiever's Edge'

'The Achiever's Edge' is my monthly audio newsletter, specifically designed to help you maximise your potential. For a FREE infopack giving you all the details you need (including major Free Bonus items) simply complete the form below and fax or post it to me.

Yes! please send me a FREE infopack with full details of the bonus items on: – *'The Achiever's Edge!'*	
Name	
Address	
Address	
Address	Postcode

Return to
Peter Thomson Ref: TPP
P O Box 666 Leamington Spa United Kingdom
CV32 6YP
Tel +44 (0) 1926 339901 Fax: +44 (0) 1926 339139

'Putting the Pinnacle Principle to Work . . . in Your Business!'

All of our Business Development Programmes are based on the 'Pinnacle Principle'. If you would like ***FREE INFORMATION*** on our in-house Business Development, Sales Development and Customer Service Development programmes, please indicate by ticking the appropriate boxes in the section below:

☐ ***Business Development***
- *Leadership and Management Skills*
- *Marketing Strategies*
- *Strategies for Business Growth*

☐ ***Sales Development***
- *Selling Skills*
- *Effective Client Relationships*
- *Sales Management*

☐ ***Customer Service Development***
- *Service Skills*
- *Service Processes*
- *Service Management*

Please also fully complete the '***Your Details***' section at the bottom of this form and send it to ***Results International plc***, at the address below. By fully completing '***Your Details***', you will ensure that we can contact you for your *FREE* consultancy session to review your full business development needs. Every form returned will entitle you to a ***FREE AUDIO TAPE by Peter Thomson*** entitled '***Business Breakthroughs***', which will provide you with the following information:

- A key thought for ***Maximising Business, Sales and Profit!***
- An amusing attitude story entitled '***Once upon a time there were two frogs . . .***'
- Details of in-house programmes and Open Seminars

If you would like details of Peter Thomson as a guest speaker for your in-house seminars or conferences, please tick the following box: ☐

Your details – please complete ALL of the following boxes:

Name:	***Business Type:***
Position:	***Manufacturing*** ***Process*** ***Service*** ***Information Technology*** ***Finance*** ***Other***
Company:	
Address:	***No. of Staff: 1–10, 10–50, 50–100, 100+***
Town:	***How many Staff need training?***
County:	***Telephone:***
Postcode:	***Fax:***
	Ref. PP1998